"This place called Africa. You think you know it. You have learned about it in school. You have come across stories about it in the media. Perhaps, you have visited the place or better still live there and so you feel that you really know it. It is not until you pick up a book that you realize that you probably do not know this place called Africa – its many countries and peoples, its multitudes of languages and experiences, its overwhelming diversity and vibrancy – as well as you think you do. And that is the beauty and joy of reading African Literature – the constant discovery."

**SIPHIWE GLORIA NDLOVU,**
author of *The Quality of Mercy*

# AFRICAN SMALL PUBLISHERS CATALOGUE

## 2024

Edited and compiled by COLLEEN HIGGS with
CASSANDRA SCHEEPERS & JESSIE COOPER

*African Small Publishers Catalogue 2024*

First published by Modjaji Books in 2024
www.modjajibooks.co.za
info@modjajibooks.co.za

Individual listings, adverts and articles © the contributors.
All other text © Modjaji Books.

All rights reserved.
No part of this book may be reproduced or transmitted in any form
or by any electronic or mechanical means, including photocopying
and recording, or any other information storage or retrieval system,
without written permission from the publisher.

Edited and compiled by Colleen Higgs,
Cassandra Scheepers and Jessie Cooper
Cover design by STOEP Collective
Cover layout & tyepsetting by Monique Cleghorn

ISBN (Print): 978-1-991240-41-5
ISBN (ebook): 978-1-991240-43-9

The printing of this catalogue kindly sponsored by:

**Bidvest** DATA
DIGITAL PRINT & PUBLISHING+

# CONTENTS

**7 INTRODUCTION**

**9 ABOUT THE EDITORIAL TEAM**

**11 LISTINGS A-Z:**

Aerial publishing 13 ... Afram Publications (Ghana) Ltd 14
African Literary Agency 17 ... African Sun Press 18
AkooBooks Ltd 19 ... AmaBooks 20 ... Amalion 22
Atypical Books 23 ... Basler Afrika Bibliographien
Publishing House 26 ... Bhiyoza Publishers Pty Ltd 27
BK Publishing Pty Ltd 28 ... Book Dash 29 ... Botsotso 31
Burnet Media 32 ... Catalogus 33 ... Catalyst Press 34
David Philip t/a New Africa Books 35 ... Deep South 36
Dryad Press 37 ... Éditions Graines de Pensées 38
Editora Trinta Zero Nove 39 ... elyzad 40
En Toutes Lettres 41 ... Femrite – Uganda Women
Writers Association 42 ... Hands-on Books 43
Harry's 44 ... Healing Prayer Press 46 ... Ibua Publishing 49
Impepho press 50 ... Inkani Books 51 ... iwalewebooks 52
Jacana Literary Foundation 55 ... Jacana Media 56
Junkets Publisher 57 ... Khaloza Books 58 ... Logos Open
Culture 60 ... Mirari Press 61 ... Modjaji Books 62
Narrative Landscape Press Ltd 64 ... Otto Foundation 67
Paperworth Books 68 ... Parrésia Publishers Ltd 69
Pelmo Book Publishers 70 ... Poetree Publications 71

Puku Children's Literature Foundation **74**
Pulani Press **75** ... Radical Books Collective **76**
Sefsasa Culture & Publishing **79** ... Sentinel Creatives **80**
The Lennon-Ritchie Agency **81** ... Tracey McDonald
Publishers Pty Ltd **84** ... Uhlanga **86** ... UNAM Press **87**

## **89** CLASSIFIEDS

## **95** ARTICLES:

Of graphite heroes and chest clothing:
the perils of self-publishing **97**

Self-publishing: A real choice for writers **101**

Imprint Africa: conversations with African
women publishers **105**

Five writers and publishers discuss the continent's
boundless literary landscape **108**

The End of an Era: Celebrating Three Vital
African Presses **117**

New Contrast literary journal **120**

#ReadingAfrica **123**

The Island Prize **127**

The Aerial publishing story **129**

## INTRODUCTION

Welcome to the sixth edition of the African Small Publishers Catalogue, a testament to the resilience and creativity of independent publishing across the continent.

This catalogue connects African publishers with a global audience and fosters vital networks within the continent itself. It's a tool for African publishers, booksellers, and literary professionals to discover and collaborate with peers across borders, strengthening the pan-African publishing ecosystem.

Our mission is to highlight small, independent publishers who play a role in nurturing local talent, preserving cultural heritage, and advancing literary innovation. It's crucial to acknowledge the formidable challenges faced by independent publishers in Africa. Financial constraints, distribution hurdles, competition from multinational publishers, and sometimes political instability pose significant obstacles. Yet, the publishers featured here persist, driven by passion and belief in their work. We appreciate their commitment to fostering a vibrant, diverse publishing ecosystem in Africa.

It is still weighted with many more South African publishers, but each time we have brought out a new edition we increase the number of publishers from across the continent.

Within these pages, you'll find brief descriptions of each publisher's work, which offers a window into the genres and subjects they cover.

We've included articles that delve into the world of independent publishing in Africa, offering context to the challenges and triumphs of this vital industry. These pieces provide insightful perspectives on the state of publishing across the continent, emerging trends, and the cultural significance of the work.

As you explore this catalogue, remember each listing represents a gateway to a world of stories, ideas, and perspectives that might otherwise remain undiscovered. Whether you're a fellow African publisher looking to collaborate, a librarian diversifying your collection, a bookseller seeking unique titles, or an educator searching for culturally relevant materials, we hope this catalogue serves as a valuable resource and source of inspiration.

Let's celebrate and support independent publishers across Africa, strengthening connections within the continent and beyond, as their success is crucial for the flourishing of African literature and knowledge in all its diversity.

We're grateful to the larger publishers, industry partners, and individuals whose advertisements and page sponsorships support this catalogue, allowing us to distribute it widely and freely.

## ABOUT THE EDITORIAL TEAM

**Colleen Higgs** is a publisher and writer, who lives in Cape Town. She started Modjaji Books in 2007, and still works there as the publisher. Her most recent book is a memoir, *my mother, my madness* (deep south) which came out in 2020. Higgs is a publishing activist, and this catalogue is one of the ways she contributes to book development and raising the profile of independent publishing in Africa.

**Jessie Cooper** is a recent postgraduate student specialising in the Study of Religions, now working as a freelance copywriter and editor. She has a diverse copywriting portfolio that includes content for coaching businesses and wellness brands, as well as social media content. Jessie's editing expertise spans academic documents and marketing materials.

**Cassandra Scheepers** is a UCT student doing her honours in Media Theory & Practice. With a background in Journalism, English literature, and Philosophy from Rhodes, she is a budding writer and junior designer with a strong love for books and culture. She edits for the online publication *Her Campus* and has been published in the *Mail & Guardian*.

# LISTINGS

# AERIAL PUBLISHING
South Africa

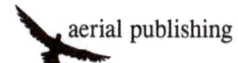

📍 c/o The Institute for the Study of the Englishes of Africa, Rhodes University, Makhanda

✉ PO Box 319, Makhanda 6140

@ aerial.publishing.grahamstown@gmail.com

☏ +27 82 928 8671

Aerial Publishing is a Makhanda/Grahamstown-based community publishing venture. We started in 2002, and have published 22 books to date, mainly of poetry. We grew out of the informal evening course that has run since 1998 at the ISEA, Rhodes University's Institute for the Study of the Englishes of Africa.

Please contact us for a pricelist. Our most recent books are two anthologies - prose and poetry - featuring 80 writers and teachers who over the years have completed or taught on the course.

If you live in Makhanda, let us know if you are interested in attending the course.

## AFRAM PUBLICATIONS (GHANA) LTD
Ghana

- C184/22 Midway Lane, Abofu-Achimota
- PO Box M18 Accra-Ghana
- aframpubghana.com
- +233 244314103
- aframpub  AframPub  aframpub

Afram Publications, a leading book publisher in Ghana, offers diverse literature and educational resources in English and indigenous languages. We specialize in promoting Ghanaian languages and culture through our publications.

Our educational textbooks cater to preschool through tertiary levels, meeting the needs of students and educators. Our commitment to quality has earned us recognition from readers, parents, and the international community.

With over 1000 titles, our catalogue includes:
- Novels and short stories in English and local languages (Twi, Ga, Ewe)
- Poetry, drama, and children's literature
- Educational textbooks and resources
- Cultural heritage materials

Our online platform makes books accessible worldwide. Join Afram's community and discover the joy of reading.

# Showcasing Ghanaian rich culture through vibrant stories.

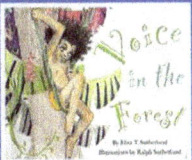

🌐 www.aframpubghana.com

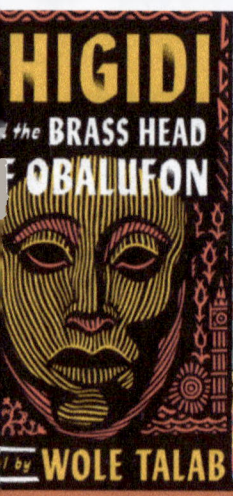

African Literary Agency connects emerging African writers with global publishers. We specialize in African Speculative Fiction, Science Fiction, Fantasy, Horror, and Children's literature.

With 20 years of expertise from our team of scouts and editors, we showcase the continent's best stories to a worldwide audience.

Find out more: www.africanliteraryagency.com

# AFRICAN LITERARY AGENCY
Ghana

@ bieke@africanliteraryagency.com
🌐 africanliteraryagency.com
👤 Bieke Van Aggelen
f African Literary Agency   📷 africanliteraryagency

African Literary Agency is a literary agency working with a premium group of books, authors, and publishers. We have been selecting emerging authors from the African continent for the past ten years, and successfully work with African fiction, Speculative Fiction mainly Science Fiction, Fantasy and Horror, Children's books, and non-fiction.

We tirelessly search for the best match between author and publisher on a global scale. Together with a team of scouts and editors, African Literary Agency works to empower African voices in literature, bringing the best stories, from all over the continent, to the readers.

# AFRICAN SUN PRESS
South Africa

- 3 Florida Road, Vredehoek, Cape Town 8001
- afpress@iafrica.com
- afsun.co.za; patriciaschonstein.com
- +27 721 844 600 : Patricia Schonstein

African Sun Press is the leading, independent publisher of poetry anthologies in South Africa. We are associates of Poetry in McGregor through whom we present the annual *Patricia Schonstein Poetry in McGregor Award*. We are also associates of The Global Empathy Project.

We publish storybooks and poetry books for children which inspire care of the Earth, a love of nature, and peace.

We administer the publishing rights of Don Pinnock and Patricia Schonstein and curate the Pinnock Photographic Archive.

## AKOOBOOKS LIMITED
Ghana

- 12C Soula Close, Labone, Accra
- POB LG 646, Legon, Accra
- ama.dadson@akoobooks.com
- akoobooks.com
- +233 202040176; +233 244012670 : Ama Dadson
- akoobooks  akoobooks  akoobooks  akoobooks

AkooBooks Audio, established in 2018, is West Africa's first dedicated audiobook publisher and digital streaming platform focusing on Black and African content. Our diverse audio catalogue features titles in English, French, and African languages across various genres, including literature, history, memoirs, and romance. We're committed to combatting illiteracy in Africa through audio storytelling and by engaging indigenous narrators who authentically portray African voices and experiences. Our audiobook productions have been Audie Awards finalists and received praise from Kirkus Reviews. In 2025, AkooBooks will produce audio versions of the Apollo Africa series from Bloomsbury UK, featuring 100 titles from the historic Heinemann African Writers Series. The Apollo Africa Audio series brings these iconic works to life aurally with contemporary African narrators, preserving and celebrating African literary heritage through the spoken word.

# AMABOOKS
Zimbabwe

✉ Crug Bychan, Ferwig, Cardigan, SA43 1PU, UK
@ amabooksbyo@gmail.com
🌐 amabooksbyo.blogspot.com
📞 +44 1239 621841 : Jane Morris
ⓕ amaBooks

amaBooks is a small, independent publisher of Zimbabwean novels, short stories and poetry, with a few local history and culture titles. We strive to produce texts that reflect the society in which the writers live, concentrating on literary fiction in English that opens windows on the history and culture of Zimbabwe. Since our inception in 2000 we have published work by over 200 writers. The rights to our titles have been acquired for the UK, USA, Canada, Egypt, South Africa, Kenya and Nigeria, and several have achieved recognition both nationally and internationally.

# AN ANNUAL CELEBRATION OF ALL THINGS LITERATURE, EVERY LITERACY MONTH OF SEPTEMBER.

BOOK LAUNCHES AND TALKS, BOOK EXHIBITIONS, WRITING WORKSHOPS AND A CHILDREN'S CORNER.

**CENTRAL BOOK FESTIVAL**

## BRINGING TOGETHER AUTHORS, PUBLISHERS, AND READERS.

YOU CAN FIND MORE INFORMATION ABOUT OUR AUTHORS AND PROGRAM ON OUR FACEBOOK.

 omoolebooks100@gmail.com   @Central Book Festival   +27 73 648 7050

**AMALION**
Senegal

- 133 Cité Assemblée Ouakam BP 5637, Dakar-Fann 10700, Dakar
- publish@amalion.net
- amalion.net
- +221 76 906 39 36 : Sulaiman Adebowale
- AmalionPublishing   Amalion   amalionbooks

Amalion is a Dakar-based independent multilingual scholarly publisher established in 2009 with the mission to disseminate innovative knowledge on Africa to strengthen the understanding of humanity. Amalion provides a platform for authors to express new, alternative and daring perspectives and views on people, places, and issues shaping our world through monographs, non-fiction and literary writings for scholars, students, and general readers with an interest in the humanities and the social sciences on Africa. Amalion titles are distributed in France and Benelux countries by Pollen-difpop, in North America by IPG and in the United Kingdom by Central Books.

# ATYPICAL BOOKS
France

- 47 route des Pyrénées, Labatut-Rivière 65700
- ruth@ruthhartley.com / johncandruthh@yahoo.com
- ruthhartley.com / epicblogue.blogspot.com
- +33 5 62 37 53 08 (landline); + 33 6 47 73 26 10 (Ruth); +33 6 68 65 97 68 (John) : Ruth Hartley & John Corley

An independent storyteller, activist and artist in a digital world of social media and rapacious global markets, Ruth Hartley has chosen to publish under her imprint of Atypical Books. Ruth's nine books tell stories from her experiences of an extraordinary world of changes from colonialism and apartheid to post-colonialism and equal rights for humans of all ethnicities, genders and heritages. Her novels, memoirs, short stories, poems, art history and a climate change children's book are well-written evocative page turners. All are available on Amazon as eBooks and POD. Find them on www.ruthhartley.com.

# SHOWCASING

## MULTILINGUAL CHILDREN'S BOOKS
*BY NEW AFRICA BOOKS*

### Tortoise and Ostrich *By Katrina Esau*

A delightful folk tale from the Northern Karoo, which is on the Southern Border of Namibia. This is the very first children's book to feature a story for children in the N|uu language. Ouma Katrina is the only N|uu speaker in the world and she runs a N|uu language school!

This tale about Tortoise and Ostrich is written in:
- N|uu, Afrikaans and English.
- N|uu, Setswana, Afrikaans, English
- N|uu, isiXhosa, Afrikaans, English

***Children will be inspired by the wily antics of the tortoise, and the humorous illustrations by well-known artist, Stanley Grootboom.***

**Author: Ouma Katrina**

### Tiqua, the Great Warrior by Stanley Grootboom

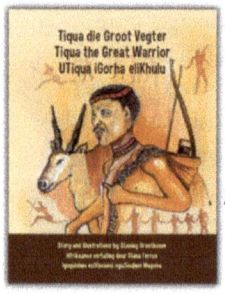

Long ago, the indigenous people of the Tsitsikamma forest knew of the healing power of the streams. Tiqua the Great Warrior was a wise chief in those times. After saving some stolen children from Gaunab the evil destroyer, he turns to the river to bring the children back to health.

**An indigenous Tsitsikamma story told in English by Stanley Grootboom, in Afrikaans by Diana Ferrus and in isiXhosa by Sindiwe Magona.**

**Author: Stanley Grootboom**

**TALK TO US**
021 467 5860
orders@newafricabooks.co.za
**www.newafricabooks.com**

*davidphilip*

***PUBLISHING BOOKS THAT MATTER — SINCE 1976***

# MULTILINGUAL MASTERPIECES BY NICOLAAS MARITZ

*Nicolaas Maritz isn't just an author; his books are vibrant works of art, making each page a joyful feast for the eyes.*

Counting begins with the basics: 1, 2, 3... This multilingual counting book showcases southern African wildlife from 1 to 10 and back again. Each number is translated into over 20 southern African languages.

The *Multilingual ABC* celebrates the linguistic diversity of southern Africa. With animal names in over 20 languages, this book invites you to embark on a journey of multilingualism—a truly empowering experience.

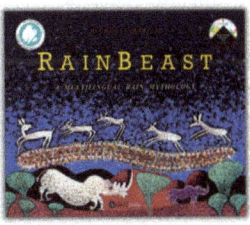

**Everyone is waiting for rain...**
See how things turn out for the local people and animals when the rain finally arrives in the drought-stricken district of Riemvasmaak.
Invigorating verse and joyful inspiration from various southern African indigenous cultures!
**Pendoring 2021 Silver Award Winner
White Raven 2022
Nominee - IBBY Honour list 2024**

**TALK TO US**
021 467 5860
orders@newafricabooks.co.za
www.newafricabooks.com

*PUBLISHING BOOKS THAT MATTER — SINCE 1976*

# BASLER AFRIKA BIBLIOGRAPHIEN PUBLISHING HOUSE
Switzerland

- Klosterberg 23, 4051 Basel
- PO Box, 4010 Basel, Switzerland
- publishing@baslerafrika.ch
- baslerafrika.ch
- +41 61 228 93 33 : Petra Kerckhoff
- baslerafrika
- basler_afrika_bibliographien

The BAB Publishing House has been publishing scholarly works on Southern Africa, especially Namibia, since 1971. Its thematic emphases are oriented towards the humanities and social sciences. The BAB Publishing House seeks to promote cultural exchange and engagement regarding important contemporary historical issues and, in particular, to provide African scholars with a platform. Our (cultural-) historical, political and anthropological publications are aimed at international academic audiences as well as engaged readers broadly interested in Africa.

# BHIYOZA PUBLISHERS (PTY) LTD

South Africa

- 📍 6443 Vermiculite Street, Ennerdale, Johannesburg 1830
- @ info@bhiyozapublishers.co.za
- 🌐 bhiyozapublishers.co.za
- 📞 +27 67 040 5029 : Menzi Thango
- 𝕏 BhiyozaL   📷 Bhiyoza_Publishers

Bhiyoza publishers is a black owned company that specialises in publishing literary books written in African languages of South Africa. The company was established in 2018 and is committed to developing African languages and preserving the history, knowledge and ideas imbedded in these languages. We are interested in publishing creative works written by African writers, in an African context, about African people, their societal issues, lifestyles, politics, education and more.

## BK PUBLISHING (PTY) LTD
South Africa

📍 1239 Francis Baard Street, Hatfield, Pretoria 0083
✉ P.O. Box 6314, Pretoria 0001  @ mail@bkpublishing.co.za
🌐 bkpublishing.co.za, supernovamagazine.co.za, preflightbooks.co.za
📞 +27 12 342 5347 : Benoit Knox
ⓕ supernovamag, PreflightBooks
ⓘ supernovamagazine, preflightbooks

BK Publishing is an independent publishing house, founded in 2005, with the aim of building a book-reading and book-buying culture in SA. Through our flagship publication, *Supernova* the mag for curious kids, we provide informative and fun reading, every two months, to help overcome reading reluctance and foster good reading habits.

Our catalogue of publications celebrates South African voices in fiction and non-fiction, with a wide variety of books for all ages and languages.

With an ever-growing well of experience in all things publishing, our expert team of language specialists, designers and project managers provides a full range of production services and solutions for local and international publishing houses and organisations. Through our imprint Preflight Books, we offer bespoke self-publishing services to help authors bring their manuscripts to life.

## **BOOK DASH**
South Africa

- @ team@bookdash.org
- 🌐 bookdash.org
- 👤 Dorette Louw
- f bookdash  ✕ bookdash  ⌾ bookdash

Book Dash is a social impact publisher of African storybooks for very young children. We champion book ownership to enrich children's home learning environments and thus increase opportunities, parental engagement and outcomes for early development. To enable that, we design and implement innovative and cost-effective models for publishing and distributing books to children at scale. Then, we work with partners to get the books to children, most often through early learning programmes. Book Dash is a registered non-profit organisation. All our books are free to read at www.bookdash.org.

# AFRICAN BOOKS COLLECTIVE

## CONNECTING YOU TO AFRICAN LITERATURE

African Books Collective (ABC) represents over 150 African publishers, showcasing a wealth of academic, literary, and diverse works. We invite new publishers in these fields to join us and become part of ABC, sharing Africa's rich stories and knowledge with the world.

AFRICANBOOKSCOLLECTIVE.COM

## BOTSOTSO
South Africa

📍 Physical address: 59 Natal St, Bellevue East, Johannesburg, 2198
@ botsotsopublishing@gmail.com
🌐 botsotso.org.za
📞 +27 82 512 8188 : Allan Kolski Horwitz
ƒ BotsotsoCollective  ✕ Botsotso_Gova  📷 botsotso_gova

*Botsotso* is a coming together of poets, writers and artists who wish to both create art as well as generate the means for its public communication and appreciation. We speak particularly of art that is of and about the varied cultures and life experiences of people in South Africa and Africa – as expressed in all our many languages – and is focussed on liberating consciousness from neo-colonial inauthenticity and elitism. We publish poetry, prose, short fiction and essays. Recent titles include Sarah Lubala's *A History of Disappearance*, Abu Bakr Solomon's *Inhabiting Love*, Sihle Ntuli's *Zabalaza Republic*, Sizakele Nkosi's *u Grand, Malume?* and David Mann's *Once Removed*.

## BURNET MEDIA
South Africa

✉ PO Box 53557, Kenilworth, Cape Town 7745
@ info@burnetmedia.co.za
🌐 burnetmedia.co.za
👤 Tim Richman
✖ BurnetMedia   📷 burnetmedia

Burnet Media is an independent publisher based in Cape Town. We produce books for two main imprints – Two Dogs and Mercury, established in 2006 and 2011 respectively – as well as various customised publishing projects. As an authors' publisher our aim is to build close and interactive relationships with our authors and clients and, in doing so, create interesting and innovative titles for South Africa and the world. Jacana Media markets our titles into the trade.

## CATALOGUS
Mozambique

**CATALOGUS**

- Karl Max, 995 – Maputo
- info@catalogus.co.mz
- catalogus.co.mz
- +258 844846486 : Mélio Tinga
- Catalogus    Catalogus

Catalogus is a platform created to project Mozambican authors to the world and to help institutions promote literary initiatives. One of its main branches is book publishing.

# CATALYST PRESS
United States

- 701 La Chapa Unit B El Paso, Texas 79912
- info@catalystpress.org
- catalystpress.org
- Jessica Powers
- catalystbooks2    catalystpress

Change can be gradual, a slight shift that over time becomes a huge movement. Or it can be quick, a frenetic burst that suddenly makes everything new. But it all begins in the same way – with a spark, a catalyst. Change begins one page at a time.

Catalyst Press was founded in 2017 as a literary spark, bringing voices from Africa to readers everywhere. We publish books that reveal the world from different perspectives and different understandings. Publishing genre and literary fiction, graphic novels, nonfiction, and books for young readers, our authors make our global community feel more connected.

# DAVID PHILIP PUBLISHERS T/A NEW AFRICA BOOKS

South Africa

- 📍 Unit 13a, Athlone Industrial Park, 10 Mymoena Crescent, Athlone Industria 2, Cape Town 7764
- ✉ PostNet Suite144, Private Bag X9190, Cape Town 8000
- @ info@newafricabooks.co.za
- 🌐 newafricabooks.co.za
- 📞 +27 21 467 5860 : Dušanka Stojaković
- f DavidPhilipPublishers  X _DavidPhilipPub  📷 newafricabooks

New Africa Books, incorporating David Philip Publishers, is one of South Africa's oldest independent publishing houses. Since the 1970s, we've built a diverse catalogue of fiction and non-fiction for all ages.

We focus on publishing children's books in all eleven official South African languages with selected titles that include sign language. Our titles have received numerous awards, including Pendoring Awards for Amonge Sinxoto's *My Big Name* and Sewela Langeni's *Making Friends with Feelings*. Other acclaimed works include Lebohang Masango's *Mpumi's Magic Beads* and several books by Nicolaas Maritz.

Our content proudly reflects African stories, and we welcome new voices like Gomolemo Moagi, Subi Bosa, Loyiso Mkize (KWEZI comics), Ouma Katrina Esau, Buhle Ngaba, Nokuthula Mazibuko Msimang, and Stanley Grootboom to our growing family.

## DEEP SOUTH
South Africa

- Firglen Farm, Highlands Road, Makhanda 6139
- PO Box 319, Makhanda 6140
- info@deepsouth.co.za    deepsouth.co.za
- +27 46 622 5081 : Robert Berold
- Deep South Publishing    DeepSouth_Books
- Deep South - YouTube

For 25 years Deep South has been publishing risk-taking South African poetry (and some prose). We look for books that will still be enjoyed and relevant in 25 years time. Writers who have published with us include Ari Sitas, Seitlhamo Motsapi, Lesego Rampolokeng, Kelwyn Sole, Mxolisi Nyezwa, Karen Press, Angifi Dladla, Joan Metelerkamp, Vonani Bila, Khulile Nxumalo, Kobus Moolman, Dimakatso Sedite, Isabella Motadinyane, Alan Finlay, Mangaliso Buzani, Haidee Kotze. Our website features contemporary reviews, articles, and interviews around each book and author.

# DRYAD PRESS
South Africa

📍 8 Durham Avenue, Cape Town, 7708
✉ Postnet Suite 281, Private Bag X16, Constantia, Cape Town 7484
@ business@dryadpress.co.za
🌐 dryadpress.co.za
📞 +27 83 408 3342 : Michèle Betty
🅕 DryadPress  📷 DryadPresssa

Dryad Press is an independent publisher dedicated to the promotion and publication of poetry in South Africa. We publish poetry, which in the words of Roland Barthes, searches for "the inalienable meaning of things". Our determinant for publication, is the ability of the literature to defamiliarise. Innovative and exciting poetry that surprises, not only in form and technique, but also in its ability to enable us to reflect on our experiences in the world in a new way. Dryad Press aims to unlock South African voices that present their stories in a fresh light and, in so doing, to nurture a new generation of South African poets.

## ÉDITIONS GRAINES DE PENSÉES
Togo

- 30 Boulevard du 13 Janvier, Nyékonakpoè – Lomé 07 B.P. 7097
- grainesdepensees@yahoo.com
- grainesdepensees.com
- +228 90 32 33 20, +228 97 36 47 47 : Mrs Yasmin Issaka-Coubageat
- editions.grainesdepensees

At Graines de Pensées, we aim to contribute to African cultural expression by publishing books that foster a democratic, pluralistic society capable of critical thinking and engagement with social issues. We are committed to providing this new generation of Africans with accessible, relatable books of exceptional editorial quality. To expand the reach of our publications, we engage in co-publishing ventures with partners in both the Global South and North. We also build strategic relationships with institutions and businesses for a better promotion of books in French, English and African languages.

# EDITORA TRINTA ZERO NOVE

Mozambique

- 1042, Amílcar Cabral Ave., Maputo 0101
- PO Box 3672, Maputo 0101
- stamele@editoratrintazeronove.org
- editoratrintazeronove.org
- +258847003009 : Sandra Tamele
- editoratrintazeronove    editoratrintazeronove
- editoratrinta9779

Editora Trinta Zero Nove (ETZN – named after September 30, International Translation Day) is a black woman-owned, independent micro publisher based in Maputo, Mozambique. It is the first Mozambican Publishing House dedicated to literary translation, and to publish audiobooks. ETZN is committed to publishing in local languages, to be innovative and inclusive in its mission to, among others, reach new readers by offering books at an affordable price that are accessible to people with disabilities. Recipients of the London Book Fair International Excellence for Literary Translation Initiatives Award in 2021, and the BOP Children's Books Publisher of the Year in Africa in 2023, in addition to being finalists of the Jabuti Award in Brazil.

## ELYZAD
Tunisia

📍 4 rue d'Alger, 1000 Tunis
@ editionselyzad@gmail.com / elyzad.leseditrices@gmail.com
🌐 elyzad.com
📞 +216 92621640 : Elisabeth Daldoul
f Éditions Elyzad   © editionselyzad   in Éditions Elyzad

Nées à Tunis en 2005, les éditions Elyzad publient principalement de la fiction, en langue française. Regards posés sur la société arabe, écritures nomades habitées par l'ailleurs, de la Mauritanie à la Palestine, les éditions Elyzad se veulent un espace de découvertes et d'enrichissement pour un lectorat curieux de textes d'auteurs africains et méditerranéens. Des livres qui explorent des horizons nouveaux, donnent à lire le monde pour le penser autrement.

Plusieurs publications ont reçu des prix littéraires en Tunisie, en France, en Italie, en Inde, au Mali, en Suisse. Le prix Alioune Diop de l'édition africaine a été décerné à la maison d'édition.

# EN TOUTES LETTRES
Morocco

📍 28 avenue des F.A.R., app. 59 - 20000 Casablanca
@ info@etlettres.com
🌐 etlettres.com
📞 +212 5 22 29 68 48 : Kenza Sefrioui

Ⓕ etlettres   Ⓧ Etlettres   Ⓘ etlettres   Ⓛ etlettres

En toutes lettres, member of the International Alliance of Independent Publishers, is an independent press specializing in the publication of essays and other nonfiction by writers, researchers, and journalists. Our books delve into social and cultural issues related to Morocco. They also promote investigative journalism in the hopes of rendering the work of researchers and academics accessible to the general public and thus spreading a culture of critical thinking and critical conversation.

En toutes lettres also runs Openchabab, which trains young journalists and civil society activists in the foundational values of a humanist society.

# FEMRITE – UGANDA WOMEN WRITERS ASSOCIATION
Uganda

✉ P.O Box 705, Kampala
@ info@femrite.org / info.femrite@gmail.com
☎ +256 772 743943 : Hilda Twongyeirwe
✖ femritewriters

FEMRITE, the Uganda Women Writers' Association, is a pioneering literary organization established in 1995. Focused primarily on empowering women writers, FEMRITE publishes both fiction and nonfiction works. The organization's core mission involves training women in writing, publishing their creative works, and promoting their voices in literature. While women's issues remain central to FEMRITE's purpose, the organization has expanded to include some programs for all writers, addressing shared challenges like limited publishing opportunities. FEMRITE actively works to nurture a vibrant literary culture in Uganda, amplifying diverse voices and stories that might otherwise go unheard.

# HANDS-ON BOOKS
South Africa

📍 50 Geluks Road, Sybrand Park, Cape Town 7700
@ info@modjajibooks.co.za
🌐 modjajibooks.co.za /genres/hands-on/
🌐 africanbookscollective.com/publishers/hands-on-books
📞 +27 72 774 3546 : Colleen Higgs

Hands-On Books is an imprint of Modjaji Books. We make beautiful books and assist you with editing, design, proofreading, printing and PR – all the things you need to successfully publish your book. We can also offer distribution into the South African and international markets.

Other services available are manuscript assessment, individual consultations about publishing, referrals to editors and ghostwriters, creative writing workshops, story-telling workshops and seminars on publishing options and how to publish successfully in South Africa.

Authors we have worked with include Kelwyn Sole, Andries du Toit, Keith Gottschalk, Jenny Hobbs, Janet van Eeden, Elizabeth Trew and Barbara Fairhead.

# HARRY'S
South Africa

📍 2 Donald Road, Vincent, East London
✉ P.O. Box 1168, East London 5201
@ poonam@harrysprinters.com
🌐 harrys.co.za
📞 +27 43 051 2440 : Poonam Harry
f HarrysVincentEL   © harrys_vincent_eastlondon

Harry's is a 95-year-old family business founded in East London, South Africa. With deep roots in publishing, Harry's believes that everyone has a story to share and is passionate about sharing local knowledge and wisdom. We publish local authors' fiction and non-fiction books through our print-on-demand model. We can print from one to many and offer a full in-house service of editing, translations, design, publishing as well as marketing and distribution. We have published children's books, novels, history books, bibliographies, educational materials, poetry and short prose to name a few. Contact us today to bring your story alive!

**ARE YOU AN ASPIRING WRITER?**

**LET US HELP YOU TELL YOUR STORY...**

## Harry's is here to assist local authors through every step:

- ☑ Book printing
- ☑ Design and layout
- ☑ Editing and translations
- ☑ Book launches
- ☑ Distribution
- ☑ Marketing

Publishing is deeply rooted in the history of our company, dating back to 1948 when Mohan Harry acquired a hand-held press and began publishing the spiritual writings of his father and the founder of Harry's, Lalloo Harry.

**EST 1929**
# 95 YEARS

As the first and only African member of the IPN Global, an alliance of friends representing leading-edge companies in the digital communications, printing, visual communications and graphic arts industry, you can be assured of exceptional quality of products and services that meet international standards.

*With over 95 years experience and expertise and branches across South Africa, Harry's is the perfect partner for your business.*

# Harry's
*Innovating since 1929*
www.harrys.co.za

East London | Gqeberha | Tshwane

**PRINTING** **BRANDING** **DESIGN** **MARKETING** **PUBLISHING** **STATIONERY**

# HEALING PRAYER PRESS
South Africa

**HEALING PRAYER PRESS**

- Rondebosch, Cape Town
- peterem@mweb.co.za / epr.healingprayerpress@gmail.com
- elizabethpeterross.com
- +27 83 448 7353 : Dr Elizabeth Peter-Ross

The Healing Prayer Press is a new company begun in 2023. 'Healing' indicates the inspiration that drives my writing. I write non-fiction that seeks to heal or to promote health in all spheres of life. The subject-matter consequently varies – the healing of South Africa's sick governance with a new form of democracy (*Biodemocracy*); the healing of brokenness of body and mind (*Healing Prayer*); and the fundamental requisites of marriage that couples must embrace to have an enduring union (*Ribbons of Love*). I publish my own work because I love being involved in every phase of the production of a book.

# ANNOUNCING

## the NEW TITLES in the SIYAGRUVA SERIES by NEW AFRICA BOOKS

### OVER 30 TITLES AVAILABLE IN THE SIYAGRUVA SERIES!

This series highlights the shape of new narratives, which resonate with the aspirations, dreams, and challenges with South African youth.
Get your copy today and join the Gruvers on their exciting journey through Young Adult life!

**TALK TO US**
021 467 5860
orders@newafricabooks.co.za
www.newafricabooks.com

**New Africa Books**
davidphilip

**PUBLISHING BOOKS THAT MATTER — SINCE 1976**

# EXCITING NEWS!

We are thrilled to announce our very first title in the vibrant KAAPS language - **VLYMSKÊP**

Regan se attempt ommie plattelandse liewe te ly wêkie ytie, maa kan hy allie vesoekings vannie city life hantee?
Wanne hy innie moelikheid belant, kan Shelley en Mncedisi hom help? En kannie Siyagruvers it bymekaa bring virrie SAOG-competition?

*'I'm so pleased they got to Mauritius'* – 'n Leser

Written by **Russell H Kaschula**
Translated **by Gaireyah Fredericks**

## GET READY
### *FOUR EXCITING NEW TITLES WILL BE PUBLISHED IN SEPTEMBER 2024*

**TALK TO US**
021 467 5860
orders@newafricabooks.co.za
**www.newafricabooks.com**

**New Africa Books**
*davidphilip*

**PUBLISHING BOOKS THAT MATTER — SINCE 1976**

# IBUA PUBLISHING
Uganda

- Hive Colab, Kanjokya House, Kanjokya Street
- P.O Box 26243, Kampala
- ibuapublishing@gmail.com
- ibuapublishing.com
- +256 759-846-669 : Karungi Charity Kwatampora
- ibuajournal   ibuapublishing   ibuapublishing

Ibua Publishing is a Uganda-based publishing house dedicated to amplifying African voices and building a home for African stories. We support emerging and established writers in Africa with training and editorial support to grow their craft and produce work that is competitive in global literary markets. We publish fiction, creative non-fiction, poetry, and children's stories, providing print and digital channels to global audiences that contribute to celebrating the stories of our time while cultivating a global appreciation for African literature.

## INKANI BOOKS
South Africa

- 87 de Korte Street, Braamfontein, Johannesburg 2001
- info@inkanibooks.co.za
- inkanibooks.co.za
- +27 76 035 5567 : Efemia Chela
- InkaniBooks  inkanibooks  inkanibooksza

Inkani Books is a people's movement-driven publishing house in Johannesburg, South Africa. We publish accessible books that intervene in the Battle of Ideas, and discussions around the contemporary dilemmas of humanity, with a focus on pan-African themes, Marxism, and struggles in the Global South. Inkani Books is a project of Tricontinental Pan-Africa.

# IMPEPHO PRESS
South Africa

📍 PO Box 12258, Queenswood, Pretoria 0121
@ getinfo@impephopress.co.za
🌐 impephopress.co.za
📞 +27 82 330 7249 : Sarah Godsell
f impephop  X impephop

impepho press is a Pan Africanist publishing house committed to the sincere telling of African and international stories, celebrating both the fragility and resilience of the human experience. We believe in championing brave, particularly feminist, voices committed to literary excellence.

We pride ourselves on providing our authors with the best editorial, design and promotional support as possible, irrespective of the stages in their careers. At impepho press, we serve the stories, always! Because without our stories, we would, in the words of Audre Lorde, be crumpled into other people's fantasies of us and eaten alive.

## IWALEWABOOKS
South Africa

- 34 Wimbledon Road, Brixton, Johannesburg
- info@iwalewabooks.com
- iwalewabooks.com
- Katharina Fink & Nadine Siegert
- iwalewabooks   iwalewabooks

iwalewabooks is a publishing house for art, discourse and archives. We dedicate our publications to aesthetic discourses, the politics of collecting and archiving and pleasure politics. Creating books is an aesthetic and collective endeavour. Many volumes are produced in collaboration with cultural workers, artists, collectives, activists and academics, mainly from the Global South.

# BRIDGE BOOKS

## JOBURG'S BOOKSHOP

bridgebooks.co.za
FB: bridgebookscbd
IG: @bridgebooks
X: @bridgebooksjozi

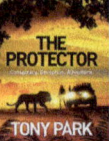

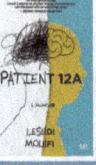
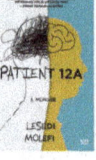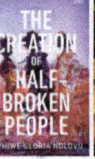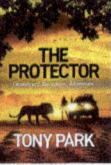

**PAN MACMILLAN SA**

**PICADOR AFRICA**

# Celebrating 20 years of African writers and storytelling.

@PAN MACMILLIAN SA    @PAN MACMILLIAN SA    @PAN MACMILLIAN SA

@PAN MACMILLIAN SA    Panmacmillian.co.za

# JACANA LITERARY FOUNDATION
South Africa

- 10 Orange Street, Sunnyside, Auckland Park, Johannesburg 2092
- PO Box 291784, Melville, Johannesburg 2109
- info@jacanaliteraryfoundation.co.za
- jacana.co.za
- +27 011 628 3200
- Jacana Media  ✕ JacanaMedia  ⓘ JacanaMedia

The Jacana Literary Foundation (JLF) is a registered non-profit company based in Johannesburg, South Africa. Established in 2013 as a way of championing fiction writers who are just beginning their careers, the JLF's mission is to promote and foster excellent writing from southern Africa.

The JLF is home to various awards and prizes: The Dinaane Debut Fiction Award, The Sol Plaatje Poetry Award and Anthology for Poetry (in all eleven South African official languages) and the Gerald Kraak Prize for Writing and Photography of African Perspectives on Gender, Social Justice, and Sexuality – the latter of which is the only prize that covers all forms of writing and printable art on the African continent. Books that emerge from the various awards are published by JLF's book publishing partner, Jacana Media.

## JACANA MEDIA
South Africa

INDEPENDENT PUBLISHING SINCE 2002

- 10 Orange Street, Sunnyside, Auckland Park, Johannesburg 2092
- PO Box 291784, Melville, Johannesburg 2109
- marketing@jacana.co.za
- jacana.co.za
- +27 011 628 3200
- Jacana Media  ✖ JacanaMedia  JacanaMedia

Jacana Media is an independent publishing house founded in 2002. It is a public interest, and frequently oppositional, publisher with a mission to assist social change, enrich public discourse and amplify progressive voices in order to create a more inclusive, just and equitable country. Jacana's non-fiction publishing focuses on, amongst many others, issues ofpoverty, race, justice, land, redress, decoloniality, colonialism, apartheid and the environment. Since their inception they have created new markets to publish for and distribute in in southern Africa and through public and media engagement they have shifted South African narratives for the greater good. Jacana Media is critically seen as a home for the nation's leading progressive thinkers, journalists, academics, activists, debut novelists, and old and new authors.

# JUNKETS PUBLISHER
South Africa

✉ PO Box 38040, Pinelands, Cape Town 7430
@ info.junkets@iafrica.com
🌐 junkets.co.za
📞 +27 78 763 3177 (Andi Mgibantaka)
ⓕ Junkets Publishers  ⓘ junketspublisher

Junkets Publisher is a small independent publisher specialising in high-quality, low-cost new South African plays. We publish the Playscript Series of individual plays, and the Collected Series of anthologies of plays. The BaxterJunkets Series publishes the winning play or the Best Script of the annual Zabalaza Theatre Festival. The UJ-Junkets Series is a collaboration with the University of Johannesburg Arts & Culture. In the near future we will inaugurate the Authors Series, collected works covering a single author's career. GayJunkets publishes queer-interest books in various genres. The first book we published in 2005 was *Rebel Angel*, a novel based on the life of John Keats. 'Junkets' was Leigh Hunt's nickname for him: 'Jun Kets'. Our logo is Keats's autograph.

## KHALOZA BOOKS
South Africa

- 6 Frolich Street, Parys, Free State
- PO Box 998, Parys, Free State 9585
- readwriteafrican@gmail.com
- khalozabooks.com
- Thato Motaung
- KhalozaBooks  KhalozaBooks  KhalozaBooks

Khaloza Books was established in 2017, as a Pan-African publishing house for books – fiction and non-fiction – about Africa for children and young adults. We are passionate about capturing, and promoting African stories in our indigenous languages, because we believe that as Africans we need to take ownership of our own narratives, and enforce a culture of reading and writing. Join us as we #ReadWriteAfrican

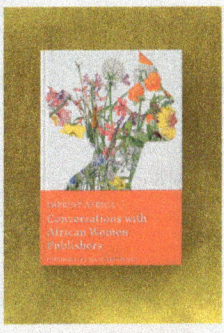

# WANT A SPINE BENDING BOOK COVER?

THEN HIRE US.

stoep
COLLECTIVE

hello@stoepcollective.com
www.stoepcollective.com

# LOGOS OPEN CULTURE
Malawi

📍 Chambo Market Bookshop and Art Gallery, Old Town Mall, off Paul Kagame Road, Lilongwe 207204

✉ P.O Box 30906, Lilongwe

@ muti@logosmw.org

🌐 logosmw.org

📞 +265 99 63 76 788 : Mutisunge Michael Etter-Phoya

(f) lovesMalawi   (ig) chambomarket   (in) logos-open-culture

We are storytellers and Malawi is our story. We use data, technology, art and research to craft and curate content on Malawi. We run Chambo Market Bookshop and Art Gallery at Old Town Mall in Lilongwe.

We are the publisher of lyrical *'Madonna is our Mother': Notes from Malawi* (Muti Michael Phoya), seminal *Making Music in Malawi* (John Lwanda), ground-breaking *Lomathinda: Rose Chibambo Speaks* (Timwa Lipenga) and best-selling *Malawi – A Place Apart* (Asbjorn Eidhammer).

# MIRARI PRESS
South Africa

⊙ 22 Delheim Road, Table View, Cape Town
@ hello@miraripress.com
⊕ miraripress.com
ⓕ Mirari Press   ⓘ miraripress

Mirari Press publishes speculative fiction with a focus on fantasy and science fiction. Speculative fiction is a grossly neglected genre in publishing in South Africa, and we aim to change that. We are particularly interested in books that are set in different worlds than our own, written by underrepresented authors, and featuring queer characters. We publish hardcover limited editions of selected titles under the Arcana Editions imprint.

# MODJAJI BOOKS
South Africa

📍 50 Geluks Road, Sybrand Park 7700
@ info@modjajibooks.co.za
🌐 modjajibooks.co.za
📞 +27 72 774 3546 : Colleen Higgs
f Modjajibooks  📷 modjajibooks

Modjaji Books is an independent feminist press based in Cape Town and a member of the International Alliance of Independent Publishers. We publish books by southern African women writers – novels, short stories, memoir, biography, poetry, essays, narrative non-fiction by women writers.

The history of publishing in South Africa is enmeshed with the culture of resistance that flourished under apartheid.

We continue to promote local women's voices, and are pleased to note that this focus has now been taken up by most trade publishers in South Africa. Modjaji titles are true to the spirit of Modjaji, the rain queen: a powerful female force for good, growth, new life, regeneration.

Our books are distributed locally by Protea Boekehuis into the trade. African Books Collective distributes our titles internationally.

*"We are the river people! We come from the depths!" Once again, true to the light and darker undercurrents of her highly creative life, Barbara's soul, like a river … is on fire."* - Ian McCallum

## THE RIVER PEOPLE

Barbara Grenfell Fairhead

T*he River People* is a multi-genre revelation of poetry, art (sculptures and beadworks), songs, interactive teachings, quotations, counsel, stories and reflections. Barbara Fairhead offers us a work that combines memoir and testimony with recent questions and learnings.

AVAILABLE FOR PURCHASE FROM
**WWW.MODJAJIBOOKS.CO.ZA**

# NARRATIVE LANDSCAPE PRESS LTD
Nigeria

📍 1B Olatunde Ayoola Avenue, Obanikoro, Lagos, Lagos State 100232

@ contact@narrativelandscape.com for general enquiries; orders@narrativelandscape.com for sales; prima@narrativelandscape.com for publishing service enquiries; and submissions@narrativelandscape.com for submissions

🌐 narrativelandscape.com   📞 +234 909 055 4407

f NarrativeLS   ✕ narrativelscape   📷 narrativelscape

Narrative Landscape Press Limited (NLP) is an independent press from Lagos, Nigeria. They believe that owning the means of production is essential to a vibrant publishing industry. To this company, the "means of production" does not just mean the printing of physical books but also implies editorial independence and book creation expertise. NLP are developing a cadre of excellent writers who work in the genres of fiction and creative nonfiction.

# W P S
## WITS PUBLISHING STUDIES

The University of Witwatersrand offers postgraduate publishing courses for Honours, Masters and PhD candidates. We equip graduate students with skills needed for publishing and offer those already in publishing an opportunity to upskill with specialist and accredited courses.

The program focuses on giving its students practical knowledge and skills in the commissioning, marketing, and editing processes while also building a nuanced understanding of the publishing environment

Contact *Laetitia.Cassells@wits.ac.za* for more information.

# Enhance Literacy with The Otto Foundation

The Otto Foundation works to improve literacy outcomes by strengthening school reading cultures and promoting reading for pleasure. We have a particular focus on promoting contextually relevant books for African children.

We manage a cluster of libraries that serve over 3000 learners in District Six, Cape Town. In 2023 our learners checked out 35344 books, we hosted 39 author readings, and each of our librarians hosted more than 256 library lessons

We invite you to visit us and share your story with a community of enthusiastic young readers!

Contact us:
info@ottofoundation.org

Follow us:

 ottofoundationSA

 @ottofoundation

# OTTO FOUNDATION
South Africa

◉ Otto Foundation Cottage, 2 Cambridge St, District Six, Cape Town 7925
✉ PSG Wealth Office, 8th Floor, 80 Strand St, Cape Town 8002
@ info@ottofoundation.org
🌐 ottofoundation.org
📞 +27 82 938 7043 : Frouwien Bosman
f ottofoundation   📷 ottofoundationSA

The Otto Foundation is dedicated to creating and managing vibrant libraries and dynamic reading programs at a cluster of schools in District Six, Cape Town. With a mission to nurture a deep love for reading and cultivate a rich reading culture in school communities, we aim to inspire young minds not only to explore the world through books but also to express their creativity by crafting their own stories. Our latest publication, *The Reading Journey*, is a captivating journal designed for children to embark on their own literary adventures. This journal, guided by a cast of whimsical furry and feathered characters, invites children to discover the joy of storytelling while developing both their reading and writing skills.

# PAPERWORTH BOOKS
Nigeria

📍 1152 Adamu Aliero Crescent, Guzape Abuja
@ info@paperworthbooks.com
🌐 paperworthbooks.com
📞 +23 48 02 313 0116 : Ibiso Graham-Douglas
ⓕ paperworthbooks  ⓧ paperworthbooks  ⓘ paperworthbooks

Paperworth Books is an independent publisher based in Nigeria. Established in 2002 as a bookshop, we have evolved to publish authentic and unique voices in Nigerian fiction, seeking to mainstream marginalised voices. We also publish narrative non-fiction, including biographies, memoirs, and history books.

Founded by Ibiso Graham-Douglas, a seasoned publisher and book industry professional with over two decades of expertise. She firmly believes in the inherent richness of African narratives, considering them fundamentally universal and complete in their own right. Paperworth Books is open to partnerships and collaborations on book development, seeking to foster innovative solutions for the democratisation of learning in Africa.

# PARRÉSIA PUBLISHERS LTD
Nigeria

- 9 Oluwole Close, Canal Estate, Okota
- parresia@parresia.com.ng
- parresia.com.ng
- +2348154582178 : Azafi Omoluabi
- ParresiaPublishers  ParresiaBooks  ParresiaPublishers

Parresia is an award-winning Nigerian press that amplifies fresh voices and publishes thought-provoking literature. We nurture first-time authors and champion diverse works that challenge and inspire. Our commitment to quality and emerging talent has earned us accolades, including the NLNG Prize for Literature (2016, 2021) and the Sharjah International Prize for Fiction (2020).

We have three imprints:
1. Regium: Literary fiction and non-fiction
2. Origami: Experimental writing
3. Omode Meta: Children's and young adult literature

By introducing readers to a new generation of Nigerian writers, we contribute to the rich tapestry of African literature and foster cultural exchange, while publishing tomorrow's classics.

# PELMO BOOK PUBLISHERS
South Africa

- 202 Gary Avenue, Waterkloof Glen, Pretoria 0181
- PO Box 10922, Centurion 0046
- info@pelmobooks.co.za / nkemi@pelmobooks.co.za
- pelmopublishers.co.za
- +27 67 152 8413 : Nkemi Molefe
- Pelmo Publishers   pelmopublishers   Pelmopublishers2141

Pelmo Book Publishers, founded in 2012 by Nkemiseng (Nkemi) Molefe in Pretoria, South Africa, originated from her desire to organise her father Dr. Lawrence Molefe's manuscripts. The company has since grown, publishing over 65 titles and representing 29 authors. Committed to preserving South Africa's linguistic diversity, Pelmo Book Publishers plays a vital role in advancing literacy and education by publishing books written in the indigenous languages of South Africa. Pelmo Book Publishers serves as a bridge connecting authors, readers, cultures, and languages, celebrating diversity and enriching the literary landscape of South Africa and beyond.

# POETREE PUBLICATIONS
South Africa

◉ 22 Visser Street, Vorna Valley, Johannesburg
@ info@poetreepublications.co.za
⊕ poetreepublications.co.za
☏ +27 73 652 0275 : Selome Motaung (Flow Wellington)
(f) poetreepub   (◎) the_poetree

Poetree Publications strives to provide affordable and accessible publishing services to writers of all genres, and change the perceptions of self-publishing as a whole. Our mission is to make a significant contribution to the publication of new work by African writers, especially African literature titles. Poetree aims to immortalise and preserve the stories and indigenous languages of writers, especially the youth, by offering self-publishing services for poetry, fiction/non-fiction, children's stories, motivational books, short stories and more. Services include publishing in print and e-formats.

# EASY READERS

## TODDLER BOOKS by NEW AFRICA BOOKS
*AVAILABLE IN ALL 11 SOUTH AFRICAN LANGUAGES*

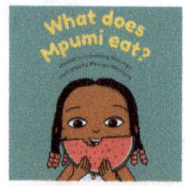

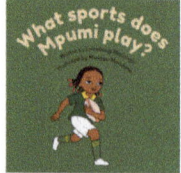

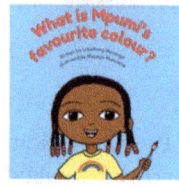

**AUTHOR:
LEBOHANG MASANGO**

**ILLUSTRATOR:
MASEGO MORULANE**

### An exciting addition to the Mpumi range!

These books are aimed at younger children and feature a younger Mpumi. Masego Morulane's illustrations encourage young readers to connect with themselves and the world in which they live. The bright and cheerful images, accompanied by short bursts of text, explain our daily activities in an easy-to-understand visual language.

*These stories are a great addition to any child's reading collection—at home or at school—and are perfect for little people between the ages of 3 and 6.*

**TALK TO US**
021 467 5860
orders@newafricabooks.co.za
**www.newafricabooks.com**

*PUBLISHING BOOKS THAT MATTER — SINCE 1976*

# EXCITING NEW

## CHILDREN'S BOOKS by NEW AFRICA BOOKS
*AVAILABLE IN ALL 11 SOUTH AFRICAN LANGUAGES*

**Nomkhubulwane, African Mother Christmas**
It's December in the Valley of a Thousand Hills - a time when people return from the cities, a time for swimming in the river and playing in the sun, a time for mangoes and new clothes. Outside Durban's busy shops, Thando sees a strangely dressed man and learns that Father Christmas is a kind person who brings children presents. Will he bring Christmas presents to the children of her Valley? Or will Gogo's magical story about Nomkhubulwane the rain goddess come true?

Written by **Gcina Mhlophe** and Illustrated by **Elizabeth Pulles**

**AUTHOR: GCINA MHLOPHE**
ASTRID LINDGREN MEMORIAL
AWARD NOMINEE - 2023

**Nozincwadi, Mother of Books**
A magical tale about reading.
In Dududu village, Mrs. Zwane, a book lover who didn't learn to read, believes in the power of printed words. Though illiterate, she collects books, knowing they hold a special magic. This story follows how she inspires the village children and how a young boy gives her the greatest gift of all—the gift of reading.

Written by **Gcina Mhlophe** and Illustrated by **Elizabeth Pulles**

**ILLUSTRATOR:
ELIZABETH PULLES**

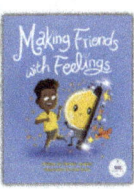

**Making Friends with Feelings**
The other kids say boys shouldn't cry ... but Lubabalo's best advice comes from a voice inside him. This voice becomes an imaginary friend who helps him to accept his emotions and feelings.

Written by **Sewela Langeni** and Illustrated by **Subi Bosa**

**PENDORING 2023 SILVER AWARD WINNER**

**AUTHOR: SEWELA LANGENI**

**Luba Goes to the Zoo**
Tata wants everyone to see some nature
-so Luba and his family visit the Jo'burg Zoo!
Join Tata, Luba, and their family on an exciting adventure to the Jo'burg Zoo!
Discover the wonders of nature through the eyes of young Luba as they explore and learn about the amazing animals that call the zoo home.
A delightful journey filled with fun and fascination for readers of all ages!
Written by **Sewela Langeni** and Illustrated by **Subi Bosa**

**ILLUSTRATOR:
SUBI BOSA**

**TALK TO US**
021 467 5860
orders@newafricabooks.co.za
www.newafricabooks.com

**New Africa Books**
*davidphilip*

**PUBLISHING BOOKS THAT MATTER — SINCE 1976**

# PUKU CHILDREN'S LITERATURE FOUNDATION
South Africa

- 136 Barry Hertzog Ave Greenside, Randburg 2193
- Postnet suite 173, Private Bag X2600, Houghton 2041
- reception@puku.co.za
- puku.co.za
- +27 671781321
- Puku.co.za   Pukubooks   Pukufoundation

Puku Children's Literature Foundation is a book development and reading promotion organisation that aims to increase access to children's literature in all South African languages, and promote literacy through its digital platforms and collaborative projects, Puku communicates, advocates, networks and participates in the promotion of books, so that authors, publishers, buyers and consumers of children's African literature content will have a more structured and organised system for selecting, reviewing and sharing accurate data on children's books.

As a strategic convenor, Puku has built unique multi-sectoral collaborations with institutions, organisations and leading experts in the education and literacy, reading promotion, book development, digital and indigenous languages ecosystems.

## PULANI PRESS
South Africa

⊙ 50 Geluks Road, Sybrand Park, Cape Town 7700
@ pulanipress@modjajibooks.co.za
⊕ modjajibooks.co.za/pulanipress
☎ +27 72 774 3546 : Colleen Higgs

Pulani Press, a new imprint of Modjaji Books, specializes in republishing and distributing selected academic titles originally released by university presses in the global north. Our mission is to make valuable scholarly works on research within the region more accessible and affordable to readers in southern Africa. The imprint launched with two significant titles: *The Work of Repair* by Thomas Cousins, an ethnographic examination of post-apartheid labour relations in South African timber plantations, and *The Politics of Potential* by Michelle Pentecost, which explores early life interventions in South Africa.

# RADICAL BOOKS COLLECTIVE

United States of America

- PO Box 770487, Steamboat Springs CO 80477
- decolonizethat@gmail.com
- radicalbookscollective.com
- Warscapes  warscapes

We build community and strengthen solidarities through conversations about books, publishing, reading and writing. We organize book clubs, events, podcasts and immersive seminars featuring radical books.

# NEW Children's Books on the Shelf!

Beautifully Illustrated Children Books by Hilma Weber, a Namibian author.

**The Treasure Hunt – A Tale of Friendship**
This is a delightful story that encourages children to appreciate the beauty of nature and the value of friendship.

**Children's Picture Atlas of Africa – An Introduction to Africa's Geography**
A visual and interactive atlas for young readers to explore the African continent. It covers the rich cultures and traditions, wildlife, and natural wonders that make Africa a truly extraordinary continent. Busy cities, villages, vibrant art, and many other features that characterize Africa are beautifully illustrated.

### Available Now!

Distributed by African Books Collective internationally.

Author contact details:
hilmaweber.na@gmail.com
www.hilma-weber.com

---

## DESKTOP PUBLISHING SERVICES

# ANDY THESEN

### FULL MEMBER OF THE PROFESSIONAL EDITORS' GUILD

• • •

EXPERIENCED COPY EDITOR, BOOK DESIGNER/TYPESETTER AND PROOFREADER. I WORK WITH FICTION AND POETRY, AND PRODUCE EBOOKS AND MANAGE BOOKS THROUGH PRINT.

• • •

ATHESEN@GLOBAL.CO.ZA        +27 082 725 8801

**TopSoilStudio**

TopSoil is a small creative studio and the lovechild of a poet and a graphic designer. We specialise in finding the visuals to compliment your words.

- Creative direction
- Illustration & cover design
- Book layout
- Promotional material

Lucienne Argent:
l.argent07@gmail.com
Sam Wells:
hello@swwwells.com

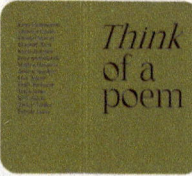

Are you transitioning from school university?

## LET THEM JUDGE YOUR BOOK BY ITS COVER.

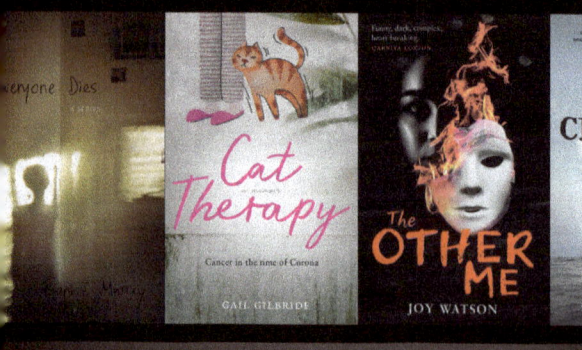

Contact MONIQUE for cover design, layout & typesetting.
**moniqueoberholzer@gmail.com**

# SEFSAFA CULTURE & PUBLISHING
Egypt

📍 49 Al-Makhzan St. Omrania, Giza 12552
@ sefsafapub@gmail.com / sefsafapr@gmail.com
🌐 sefsafa.com
📞 +20 1110787870, +20 1016948466 : Mohamed El-Baaly
f sefsafa   ✕ Sefsafapub

Sefsafa Culture & Publishing is a small group based in Egypt, working under the umbrella of 'Sefsafa Culture & Publishing'. We have had a publishing house since 2009, and have published over 400 titles, one third of them translations. The group has also organized the Cairo Literature Festival since 2015, and the Egypt Comix Week festival since 2014. Sefsafa aims to support the enlightenment and Arab Spring ideals.

# SENTINEL CREATIVES
South Africa

◉ 4 Deneys Road, Bergvliet, Cape Town 7945
@ sentinelcreatives@gmail.com
🌐 sentinelcreatives.net
👤 Scott Miller & Mitchell Lüthi
ⓕ sentinelcreatives ⓧ sentinelcreativ 📷 sentinelcreativespublishing
▶ Sentinel Creatives   Ⓡ Sentinel_Creatives

Sentinel Creatives is an indie press and production house located in Cape Town, South Africa, specialising in superb works of fiction and near-fiction.

Established in 2018, the company was founded by a small but dedicated team of like-minded individuals, with a view to producing and distributing original stories, comics, games, and other forms of media. The scope of our output has since narrowed to focus primarily on long and short-form fiction. In the relatively brief time since our inception, we've had the pleasure of working with formidable writers from all over the world, some well-established and some previously unknown, and have published several standalone novels, novellas, and short-story anthologies.

Our works are distributed in a variety of formats, both physical and digital, and our sister company, Citadel Studios, creates richly detailed audiobook adaptations of those works.

# THE LENNON-RITCHIE AGENCY

South Africa

- ✉ info@lennonliterary.com
- 🌐 lennonliterary.com
- 📞 +27 21 447 9797
- 🅕 The Lennon-Ritchie Agency   📷 lennonliterary

The Lennon-Ritchie agency is a full service literary agency with offices in Cape Town and Johannesburg, South Africa. We represent a select group of international writers of literary and commercial fiction, non-fiction, and children's literature. We represent authors and we sell International and film/TV rights on behalf of publishing houses including Penguin Random House South Africa, Pan Macmillan South Africa, Jonathan Ball Publishing, Mirari Press, Crystal Lake Publishing, and Duck Creek Press, New Zealand. And in a twist on the above, we help producer partners sell book and graphic novel rights to their projects in development. Clients include Triggerfish Animation Studios and Baboon Animation.

# CANEX BOOK FACTORY

The CANEX Book Factory is a key initiative by Africa Export-Import Bank (Afreximbank), under its CANEX Programme, to promote a vibrant literary culture across Global Africa and encourage a sustainable business ecosystem in the book value chain.

The CANEX Book Factory's year-long programme of interventions include:

» A Pan-African writing workshop to support and develop literary talent within Africa and its diaspora.
» A prestigious publishing prize in Africa that awards USD20,000 to the publisher of the best trade book and USD2,000 each to four finalists.
» A resource e-newsletter curating legal, accounting and creative writing resources for African writers, editors, agents, publishers and booksellers.

About CANEX: The Creative Africa Nexus (CANEX) was launched in 2020 to support and boost Africa's creative and cultural industries. The CANEX programmes aim to address challenges faced by the creative economy by providing a comprehensive suite of tools, including access to finance, capacity building, trade support, and investment promotion.

**Learn more about CANEX here: https://canex.africa**

Partner Organisations:
Narrative Landscape Press Limited
and
James & Grace Adichie Foundation

PROMOTED BY

IN COLLABORATION WITH

HOSTED BY ALGERIA

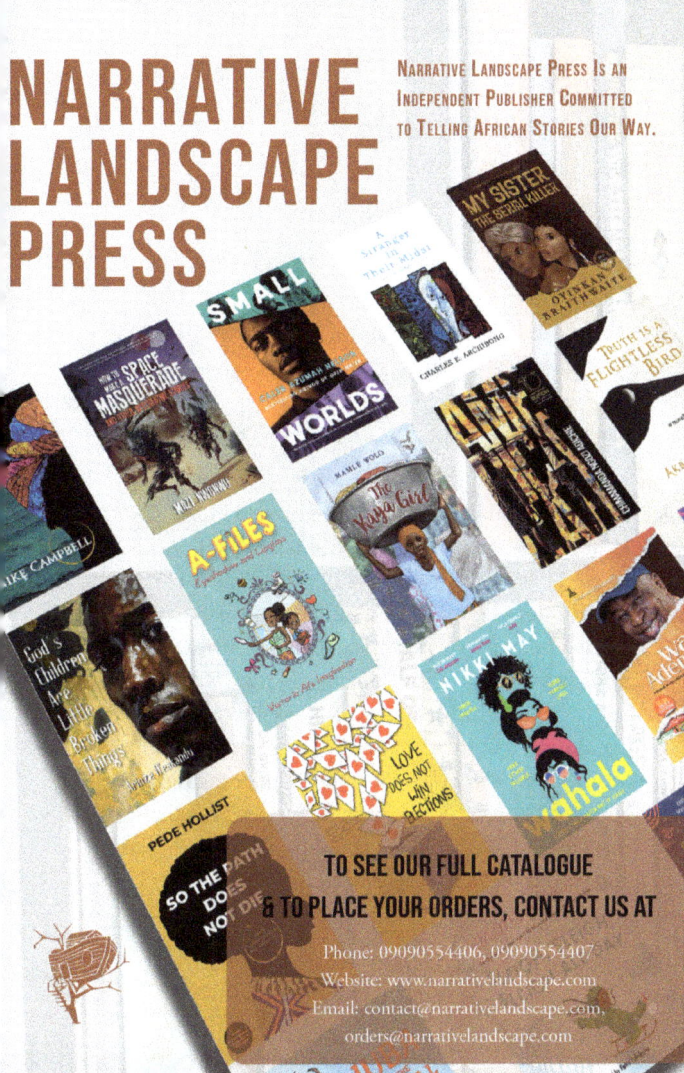

# TRACEY MCDONALD PUBLISHERS PTY LTD

South Africa

✉ Suite No. 53, Private Bag X903, Bryanston 2021
@ tracey@ilovebooks.co.za
🌐 traceymcdonaldpublishers.com
📞 +27 83 659 7489 : Tracey McDonald
ⓕ TMcDPublishers   ⓧ tmpublishers   ⓘ tmpublishers

Tracey McDonald Publishers, established in 2013, is a leading indie publishing house based in South Africa. In the 11 years of business we have published 123 titles. Under the TMP imprint we publish non-fiction titles, written by people from Africa, or about Africa. We take pride in every book, knowing that readers will finish that last page armed with knowledge, insights, ideas and inspiration that they can put into action (be it in their business, societal or personal life). Under the Incwadi Yothando imprint, we publish fiction – stories that you can relate to, stories where you grow with the characters, and stories that fill you with a range of emotions.

## UHLANGA
South Africa

⊙ Durban
@ nick@uhlangapress.co.za
⊕ uhlangapress.co.za
⊙ Nick Mulgrew
⊚ uhlangapress

uHlanga is a small South African poetry press run by Nick Mulgrew. We publish single-author collections of poetry in English and isiXhosa, as well as chapbooks and collaborations with other small presses. Our books have won most major South African and African poetry awards, including the Ingrid Jonker Prize, the South African Literary Award for Poetry and the Glenna Luschei Prize for African Poetry. Our books are taught in universities and schools around the world, and have been translated into several languages.

## UNAM PRESS
Namibia

◉ 340 Mandume Ndemufayo Ave, Pionierspark, Windhoek
✉ Private Bag 13301
@ unampress@unam.na
🌐 unam.edu.na/unam-press
📞 +264 61 2064714 : Naitsikile lizyenda
f UNAMPress    📷 unam_press

The University of Namibia Press (UNAM Press) publishes works on topics related to Namibia and the Southern African region, reflecting the strengths of the University and the best scholarship in and on Namibia and the region. Published and forthcoming titles include studies of culture and languages; nation building and democracy; education; law; social and political history; autobiographies; literature; the environment and sustainable development.

# CLASSIFIEDS

**DANYA RISTIĆ-SCHACHERL | danyaristic@gmail.com**
I am a freelance editor and proofreader specialising in poetry, fiction, narrative non-fiction, monographs and memoirs, with many years of work experience. Supported by a doctorate in English Literature and having gained the status of accredited text editor (English) at the Professional Editors' Guild, I offer meticulous, discerning, efficient and reliable service.

**JULIET GILLIES | julietg@icon.co.za / www.writeskills.co.za**
Professional editor with a post-graduate qualification in English and over 20 years of experience. I focus on more serious texts, such as academic, government and business texts. I particularly enjoy editing book manuscripts and have edited topics such as: Africa, peace & security, the blue economy, waste management, history, China in Africa, various biographies and autobiographies, gender matters, social issues, politics, government and related, and religion.

**LOUISE RAPLEY – WORD MAGICIAN | wordmagician.co.za**
I'm a talented, versatile editor and writer with great skills and years of experience. Most of all, though, I'm a human being who loves communicating and helping others get their written words out into the world.

I enjoy working on narrative non-fiction manuscripts, especially memoirs, biographies and self-help books.

Manuscript evaluation | Developmental editing
Overwriting | Copy-editing | Proofreading

**MEGAN HALL** | sleastie@gmail.com (Full CV on LinkedIn)
Focuses on: Literature; Textbooks; Dictionaries; Corporate; Scholarly
Able to research and conceptualise new products, develop proposals and costings, manage manuscript development and authors, negotiate contracts / rights, brief editors and production, draw up schedules, edit, proofread, project manage and generally make books happen.

Almost 30 years in publishing, working on a wide range of materials, and ending as publishing manager for dictionaries and literature at Oxford University Press. Freelancing since 2018 as a researcher, freelance publisher, editor, proofreader, writer etc. Comfortable with Adobe, Microsoft and Google suites as well as TshwaneLex.

**NERINE DORMAN** | nerinedorman@gmail.com
In need of a fresh pair of eyeballs on your manuscript? Have you written a sweeping fantasy epic, an action-packed space opera, or a gritty post-apocalyptic thriller? Heck, even super-spicy romance or teens solving mysteries... Nerine Dorman is not only an award-winning author, but she's been editing long enough to have Seen Things. So, be it helping you apply changes suggested in that pesky reader report that has you wailing in dismay, or even digging in with her red pen to help you snip and polish your story, she's happy to consider what your unique needs are, and tailor make her approach. With two decades' experience as both editor and author, she offers reader reports, structural edits, copy edits, ghostwriting, proofreading, and coaching. Although her preferred genres are fantasy, science fiction, historical, and horror (adult and young adult), she has extensive experience editing romance and its various subgenres.

**For her rates, see nerinedorman.blogspot.com/p/editing-rates**

**PHILLIPA MITCHELL: GHOSTWRITER, EDITOR, PUBLISHER**

We all have a story inside us waiting to be told. Perhaps it's a struggle you faced, but you chose to rise above it. Maybe it's an experience that changed your life. Or it could be wisdom you want to share.

Your story is important.

Not everyone is wired to write a book, but we all have experiences worth sharing. Your published story might inspire someone to take a leap of faith or help another to heal.

Having worked in the book industry since 1991, I can help bring your story to life. Whether it's ghostwriting, editing, consulting on publishing, or working with you to independently publish your book, I'm here to support you every step of the way.

It's time to set your story free. Let's make it happen, together.

**Visit me online at: www.phillipamitchell.com**
**Email: phillipa@phillipamitchell.com**

**SILKE HEISS**

Need creative input and feedback on your poems, literary or creative manuscript? I come highly recommended with

- 38 years of creative literary experience
- a sensitive heart
- a sharp mind
- excellent communication skills

I'd love to help you develop your work to its fullest potential.
**Email: silkeheiss@gmail.com; WhatsApp: +27 (0)66 2546846;**
**Website: silkeheiss.co.za/**

**SISTER K PUBLISHERS**
Sister K Publishers offers comprehensive services to transform your story into a compelling book. Our expertise includes coaching, editing, cover design, and distribution, ensuring your book reaches its fullest potential. Whether you need assistance clarifying your ideas, refining your manuscript, designing an eye-catching cover, or distributing your book to major retailers, our team is here to help. Share your story with the world and make a meaningful impact.
**Contact us today at sisterkpublishers@gmail.com or www.sisterkyende.org to start your journey as an author.**

**THE WORD COMPANY: Better writers. Bigger stories**
Unlock the power of language with our writing workshops. Our workshops are interactive to empower business writers to communicate with clarity and impact. Struggling to find the right words for your organisation? Our experienced copywriters can bring your brand story to life. We also provide author coaching for writers-in-a-rut.
**www.thewordcompany.co.za | writer@thewordcompany.co.za**
**+27 71 636 8028**

# ARTICLES

## OF GRAPHITE HEROES AND CHEST CLOTHING: THE PERILS OF SELF-PUBLISHING  *by Charlene Smith*

Publishers launch a million books each year, while a further three million self-publishers boost the profits of vanity presses and pay for Jeff Bezos' super-yachts.

Most of those who self-publish do not realise that the world is not waiting for your book. Once you've written it and given a substantial amount to vanity publishers to 'edit' it, and you're often lucky if they even do a Grammarly check, or you have struggled through Kindle Publishing's tools, you discover that no one hails your book but for your mum. And your best friend. Maybe.

Those who urged you to pen your masterpiece are strangely unwilling to dole out even R20 for your beautiful book. The realisation creeps in: distribution is everything. Amazon is a graveyard for self-published books. You're stuck with trying to figure out how to get your book into the hands of disinterested journalists and bookstores.

Every person who has an interesting story to tell, and journalism has taught me that everyone does, listens to friends who have never written books who say: "you should write a book." And so, they do. Or the best they can. People who get many likes on social media call themselves 'influencers,' even if they have just 2,000 followers and believe this demands a book. They are convinced millions will flow into their bank accounts. God bless their optimism.

A book distributor sometimes leafs through the novels

from vanity publishers and sends me pearls. There is the romance writer who wanted to describe her protagonist's face as chiselled like granite (cliché alert) but instead wrote, "His face was graphite," which is the writing part of pencils. Another said her female lead was identified by her "chest-clothing"– the author probably means a blouse or something funnier. I'll leave it up to your imagination.

This from a publisher: "He didn't answer but gave a heavy sigh that came from deep within, as if he was trying to exhume the whole world from himself. But it's not easy to exhume the whole world from within yourself. It is a huge, incorrigible chunk that gets stuck in your throat and keeps words trapped in the claustrophobia of your chest until, after squirming and poking, the words themselves also fall back into your viscera." Yes, well, moving on.

It is hard to get your book accepted by a commercial publisher. There are fewer book publishers worldwide than when my first book was published in 1999. In those days, publishers treated authors like royalty; they'd treat you to expensive lunches, have million-rand book launches, send limousines to fetch you at airports, and pay for first-class airfares.

Since then, there has been a bloodbath in publishing, with Penguin Random House swallowing up each other and everything in their path. Monopolies are not good for producers or consumers.

Yet, small publishers continue to emerge and, like dandelions, insist on persisting. Most will give more loving attention to your book than the big guys. J.K. Rowling, after being rejected by 12 publishers, found a tiny publisher that took a risk by publishing her.

Writing is hard work, and believing in yourself is imperative. Ernest Hemingway wrote from experience when he said, "There is nothing to writing. All you do is sit down at a typewriter and bleed." I've been a professional writer for four decades and a developmental editor for two decades, and I am still learning. The best writers worry about structure, syntax, and style. They write multiple drafts. They are hell to live with while writing a book because they become distracted. Sending a book to a publisher is agony; going on a blind date is way easier.

> Every professional writer will tell you that a book is as good as your editor

Rejection is torment, but it offers an opportunity for learning and improvement. Once your book is accepted, you will be guided by editors. But even for a journalist like me, subject to a lifetime of editing, when I receive pages back from a book editor and see the lines of red, I make myself tea and walk around the garden to find courage, then go back to the computer to do the necessary corrections.

Every professional writer will tell you that a book is as good as your editor. My worst editor told me he was thrilled to have the privilege of editing my book; he'd admired me for so long. I knew then that the book and I were in trouble. The best was a Swedish editor translating one of my books into that language. We'd have long phone conversations where he would ask, "When you wrote x, what exactly did you mean?" And I'd say,

"I have no idea." I'd put the phone down and struggle to find meaning in my writing and improve it. The magic of writing is that it links to the unconscious, so we need to interrogate that surprising thought that made its way to the page. I wish I could read Swedish because I am convinced that edition of my book is the finest.

Writing is about humility. It is also about going into bookstores, looking for books like yours, looking for the names of their publishers and daring to approach them. Now, leave your ego at the door and get down to some meaningful writing. Good luck!

**Charlene Smith** is a multi-award-winning journalist, author of 14 commercially published books, authorised biographer of Nelson Mandela, a writing teacher and developmental book editor. Born in Johannesburg, she now lives in Boston, USA.

## SELF-PUBLISHING: A REAL CHOICE FOR WRITERS

*by Jessie Cooper*

Picture this: You've poured your heart and soul into a novel, only to face a barrage of rejections from traditional publishers. Sounds like a dead end, right? Not anymore. The past ten years have seen self-publishing turning the tables on how the publishing world works.

Some examples. Jackie Phamotse's best-selling series *BARE* found its audience through self-publishing after notable publishing houses showed her the door. After too many rejections threatened to crush Tanya Meeson's spirit, she decided to take matters into her own hands and self-publish her debut novel, *The Fulcrum*. It became her way of preserving her "mental, spiritual, and emotional health." Dudu Busani Dube found bookstores clamouring for her self-published Hlomu series. The series eventually sold in the tens of thousands, a massive feat in South Africa for any book, let alone a self-published one.

But it's not just about bouncing back from rejection. Some authors, like Fiona Snyckers, have chosen to dive into self-publishing despite success with four traditionally published novels. Snyckers felt the itch to try something new. "I have always had more stories in my head than a traditional publisher could keep up with," she explains. It's this freedom and pace that draws many writers to the self-publishing path.

Self-publishing can be like being handed the keys to your own literary kingdom. You're the boss of everything – from the words on the page to the font on the cover. This control extends to your copyright, which is a big deal in an age where a book could become the next binge-worthy TV series. Self-publishing means you're not just the creative genius behind the story; you're also the CEO, project manager, marketing department, and distribution centre of your one-person publishing house.

It's also a crash course in the publishing industry, so it's not for everybody. You'll no longer have an experienced publisher advocating means for your book, and it can be tough to be your own advocate and promoter. You might find yourself making newbie mistakes. You might have blind spots about the editing or packaging of your book. The discounts of around 40% that bookstores demand could force you to rethink your pricing. Many self-published authors, in a rush of enthusiasm and blind trust, have found themselves left with a garage full of boxes of books they will struggle to sell. Getting reviews can be tougher than convincing a cat to take a bath, and you might find the shelves of major bookstores closed to you unless you do a lot of legwork and research.

There's also the stigma of not being "good enough" or "vanity publishing". Many literary awards exclude self-published work, many book festivals might not invite self-published authors. But don't let this scare you off. The self-publishing world is shaking off its stigmas and evolving, with more options than ever.

Modjaji publisher Colleen Higgs runs a separate imprint called Hands-On Books, which offers what she calls "assisted self-publishing and hybrid publishing." It's a middle ground that gives authors a lot more control and potentially more income while still providing the support and experience of a publishing house. Authors get involved in every decision, from cover design to marketing strategies, because they're footing all or part of the bill.

What to call this new breed of publishing? Higgs isn't a fan of terms like custom publishing ("sounds too corporate") or boutique publishing ("sounds like expensive small hotels"). Higgs believes hybrid publishing is the best term, as it blends elements of traditional and self-publishing. It's an approach that offers authors more support and credibility than going it alone, while still giving them a significant say in the process.

If you're thinking of dipping your toes into the self-publishing waters, here's some advice:

- Educate yourself. The publishing world can be as complex as a George R.R. Martin plot, so learn as much as you can before diving in. Build a community of fellow authors and industry pros – they'll be your lifeline when things get tough. Don't print too many copies, digital printing allows you to print 50 copies or 200 at a time, so don't risk printing 2000.
- Don't skimp on quality. Your self-published book should be able to stand shoulder-to-shoulder with anything coming out of publishing houses. That means investing in professional editing, cover design, paper quality, and marketing.
- Speaking of marketing, get ready to build your social media profile. If used mindfully it can be your route to

finding and connecting with readers. And remember, there's a massive "reader appetite" out there, especially for serialized genre fiction in the 60,000 to 80,000-word range.

At the end of the day, self-publishing is all about weighing the pros and cons. Yes, you get control and potentially higher earnings. But you're also taking on all the risk and responsibility. It's not for everyone, but if you have an entrepreneurial streak and are willing to put in the work, it can be rewarding. You might enjoy selling books from the boot of your car for one book, but the adventure of it might pale after that first few months of hand-selling each copy.

At the very least, you will learn about publishing. Self-publishing gives authors "a more realistic sense of what publishers offer when they take on a book. And how tough it is to make it work. It can be a journey of discovery, not just of the publishing world, but of yourself as a writer and entrepreneur.

# IMPRINT AFRICA: CONVERSATIONS WITH AFRICAN WOMEN PUBLISHERS

*by Joel Cabrita*

*Imprint Africa: Conversations with African Women Publishers* maps an early twenty-first century history of the remarkable women who have pioneered the publishing industry in Africa in the last few decades. These luminaries have modelled resistance to the forces excluding African writers from the publishing industry, both on the continent and beyond. Our 9 profiled publishers address themes of North-South economic disparity in the publishing industry, the demise of publishing on the continent amidst Structural Adjustment Programs and the political turmoil of the 1970s, the importance of African language publishing, the gendered dynamics of publishing in Africa, the fluid nature of African identity in an era of migration and diaspora, and the new importance of online platforms for African publishers. Featuring a preface by celebrated publisher Margaret Busby, the anthology highlights the contributions of female knowledge producers on the African continent, and it celebrates the works created, circulated, and promoted by the new network of female intellectuals and activists whom the book chronicles.

> Over the last decade, the landscape of African literature has changed dramatically

Over the last decade, the landscape of African literature has changed dramatically. The flowering of women-led publishing houses and literary festivals such as Huza Press in Rwanda and Ake Arts and Book Festival in Nigeria has led to two major literary-publishing shifts traced

A COLLABORATION BETWEEN STANFORD, MODJAJI BOOKS, HUZA PRESS, AND PAIVAPO PRESS.

'VOLUMES LIKE THIS HAVE A CRITICAL ROLE TO PERFORM IN ENSURING THAT THE GOOD NEWS, AND BEST PRACTICE, IS ALWAYS PASSED ON AND REMAINS FOUNDATIONAL'
- **MARGARET BUSBY**

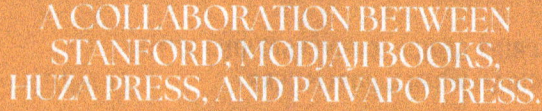

IMPRINT AFRICA
Conversations with African Women Publishers
FOREWORD BY MARGARET BUSBY

IMPRINT AFRICA is a collection of interviews that chronicles the work of a new network of female intellectuals and activists who have transformed African publishing across the twenty-first century.

by the book. First, more opportunities exist than ever before for African women to narrate their own stories; and second, a growing number of writers and publishers are now challenging the hegemony of northern hemisphere publishers in producing literary representations of the continent. Through a series of conversations with the African women who have spearheaded these changes (e.g. Goretti Kyomuhendo, founder of FEMRITE and the African Writers Trust, and Zukiswa Wanner, one of the co-founders of Afrolit Sans Frontieres as well as of Paivapa Press), *Imprint Africa* traces the inception and development of this ongoing literary movement to expand the boundaries of African literature.

Framed as a set of conversations between Joel Cabrita (Professor of African History at Stanford University), Stanford University students, and publishers from the continent, *Imprint Africa* presents the generation and preservation of knowledge as a living process – a dialogue between individuals of varying personal identities and cultural backgrounds. Not only does this allow for more expansive discussions of publishing in its various forms, but also frames the production of knowledge as an active practice that demands community engagement.

## FIVE WRITERS AND PUBLISHERS DISCUSS THE CONTINENT'S BOUNDLESS LITERARY LANDSCAPE

*Ed Nawotka Talks to Sulaiman Adebowale, Colleen Higgs, Jessica Powers, Sandra Tamele, and Rachel Zadok*

Sulaiman Adebowale (SA) is the founder and director of Amalion, an independent publishing house in Dakar, Senegal.

Colleen Higgs (CH) is publisher of Modjaji Books, an independent feminist press from South Africa.

Jessica Powers (JP) is publisher of U.S.-based Catalyst Press, which focuses on African titles.

Sandra Tamele (ST) is publisher of Thirty Zero Nine, a press dedicated to publishing translations, based in Maputo, Mozambique.

Rachel Zadok (RZ) is founder of Short Story Day Africa, an organization that creates a global platform for emerging and established African writers.

Questions were initially posed by Ed Nawotka, senior international editor of *Publishers Weekly*.

\*

### Can you tell us a little about your publishing house and its priorities?

*Sandra Tamele (ST):* Trinta Zero Nove is dedicated to literature in translation, to celebrate 30/09 international translation day, first from English and French into Portuguese, and currently from any language into the main four Moz languages: Macua, Sena, Changana and Portuguese.

***Colleen Higgs (CH):*** Modjaji Books is a small independent publishing company, with a focus on publishing southern African women writers.

***Sulaiman Adebowale (SA):*** Amalion publishes knowledge in all its forms, stories, narratives, biographies, poems, art books, monographs, etc.

***Jessica Powers (JP):*** Catalyst Press is a North American based company with worldwide distribution and we focus exclusively on African writers and African-based books. We publish children's and adult titles. We publish in all genres.

***Rachel Zadok (RZ):*** SSDA isn't a publisher in the conventional sense. We're more of a development project for African fiction writers and editors, with a publishing aspect. Our ethos is subvert, reclaim, reinvent. Subvert what it means to be an African writer, reclaim space for non-conformist African voices, and reinvent African short fiction so that writers can tell their stories without the pressure of writing to an idea of what an African story should be.

\*

**Is there something unique to the challenges you are facing in publishing in your country? What have been your solutions?**

***ST:*** There is a perceived lack of reading culture or habits that we try to counteract by publishing books our readers may find more relatable and more affordable than those by other publishers. We are pioneers in audiobook publishing and e-commerce channels with integrated MoMo.

***CH:*** Books are expensive here, partly because of this, but also paper, ink, and printing are pricey and even an excellent, highly publicized novel will only sell just over 1,000 copies. This means that a company like Modjaji has had to operate as a "subsistence" publisher. However, thanks to digital printing and social media, we are able to do more than we would have in the past and to "punch above our weight."

*SA:* The challenges peculiar to the business environment are the same for all entrepreneurs on the continent and they still manage to thrive and fail within that same environment, so the publishing sector and publishers just get on with it as well. Beyond the creative aspects to your lists, you dig into the same practical solutions other sectors use. If there are credit card issues for online commerce, you add mobile money options; if the postal system does not work and your customers find couriers too expensive, you use motorcycle delivery.

*JP:* I still think North Americans don't understand that Africa is a continent, and there are a lot of stereotypes we're fighting. We keep working to chip away at those stereotypes in part by publishing books people don't expect to see from the continent, like graphic novels; and through efforts like the annual #readingAfrica campaign.

*RZ:* South Africa has a pretty robust publishing scene but, for the most part, no one is looking to develop voices, it's more about the slick and the polished. But not everyone has had the same opportunities, and there is something incredible about looking beyond the expected for a raw spark, because craft you can teach, but that spark is what makes a voice special.

\*

**What is your perception of the impression "African" publishing is making – African is in quotes, as this is a continent with 54 countries and vastly differing publishing ecosystems?**

*ST:* As a literary translator and publisher invested in making Moz/the PALOP read their neighbors, I'm delighted with the African bibliodiversity. I only wish it was easier to build B2B bridges within the continent (often it is easier and cheaper to meet at book fairs overseas because of language barriers and the cost of traveling).

*CH:* It feels to me as if African publishing is having its Latin American moment if I can put it like that. So that is exciting, but there is a still long way to go. And even in South Africa, books in English have to compete with books published in rich northern countries like the US and UK.

*SA:* That it is important as our contribution to the creative global space of ideas and stories about ourselves and the world. That the sector continue to thrive in the myriads of publishing programs, independent, big small, corporate and the like, so as to provide options for authors to express and share ideas and stories.

*RZ:* As you say, it's a diverse continent, and it irks me that there's a section for African publishing, but not one for European publishing. I think it's far more important to push our writers and get them noticed as individuals, as writers worth reading because they're worth reading, not because they're African. This to me is how we go about changing perceptions of Africa, and start creating a connection that transcends that and begins to link reader to writer in terms of human experience, one person to another.

*SA:* Shedding restrictive labels opens up more opportunities for everyone. However, it is equally critical that we own the label "African publishing," not just because it is true, we are Africans, and if we do not others will define and (mis)represent that label for us.

Secondly, writers will actually do better across cultures if the African publishing sector is in control, including both commercially and creatively in the narratives. Our products should be seen as different from a business point of view…but also as our own contribution to the literary diversity of humanity. I love that word "bibliodiversity"!

> I love that word "bibliodiversity"!

\*

**Is there something that people consistently get wrong in discussing your publishing program or about publishing and reading culture in your country in general?**

*ST:* I will have to think about this, but I think I mentioned the misconception that Moz people don't read at all. In my opinion this is only true in richer, urban settings, but the lack of a distribution infrastructure prevents us from reaching our rural readers.

*SA:* That it is monolingual. That a Francophone country would read only in French for instance. It sounds innocuous and of legitimate concern but the assumption is from a very English-speaking perspective, e.g., how many books in French can you sell in let's say Kenya, Ethiopia, and South Africa?

*CH:* Distribution and cost of books makes access to them difficult for rural and poorer people. But as the widespread use of cellphones in Africa has revealed people do read, they find plenty to read on their phones if they are linked to the internet.

*JP:* In North America, there is a huge push for people to read "diverse" books but diverse books are defined as written by and/or about Americans of different cultural identities. So global literature isn't included in the definition of "diverse." I'd love to see North American librarians and educators embrace global literature as part of their definition of "diversity."

\*

**What are the biggest challenges you face as a member of the publishing in the "global South" dealing with the North American industry.**

*ST:* When discussing rights agreements, I'm often faced with unrealistic royalties expectations from North American authors and/or their agents. We often waste precious time until they understand our reality in terms of print runs, sales price and timelines. But overall my feeling is that the North is more keen to be published in translation in Moz than the other way round.

*CH:* The North American market seems quite distant to me. A bit like wondering how things work on Mars. If our Department of Arts and Culture took local publishing seriously, they would create a system like the one in Canada where local books that meet a certain standard would be bought in decent numbers for our libraries. I think we have about 2000 libraries in SA. What if they bought 500 copies of new titles that qualified initially? That would change everything.

I'd also really like to find a way to get our books into other African countries. It seems as if it is harder to connect with the rest of the continent than it is to connect with the West.

*SA:* I truly believe in the book trade as an essential ecosystem to be maintained and supported so as not just to get books to readers in the most efficient and cost-effective means possible, but also as part of the fabric of our collective human culture and world-view. But, and this is not just North America, including UK and Europe as well, the book trade acts like gatekeepers to what their public can and should be exposed to.

> There is much to be gained by readers knowing that they are reading African literature. It is something to feel proud of that we are African publishers

\*

### How would you like to see the narrative about African publishing and literature change globally?

*CH:* I think there is much to be gained by readers knowing that they are reading African literature. It is something to feel proud of that we are African publishers. I feel it gives us all a platform, a place from where our writers can be seen.

*SA:* By globally, if you mean generally and not as in the world, I would say to be published and read locally by millions and millions of Africans based in every nook and cranny of the continent in indigenous, local, national and global languages. It is a shame if African voices are not read by Africans as much as they continue to read others.

*JP:* I still think there's a perception that African-authored literature should somehow be "serious," literary. Many Africans are writing genre literature. Why shouldn't we have African romances, African crime novels, African thrillers?

*RZ:* Again, just stop seeing African literature and just see literature.

*SA:* Jessica, we already do have a lot of the genres cited. Writing and publishing of romance, thrillers, crime etc have been going on for decades on the continent. Certainly their successes are intertwined with the level of the money available for the production and push. That onus is on us, the publishers. If writers submit those genres and we like them, we can and should invest in them. If we cannot do it alone, there's strength in alliances and networks as Colleen and Sandra rightly noted above.

*JP:* Sulaiman, absolutely! But outside of Africa, we tend to think about African literature as "very serious," but just as Siphiwe Gloria Ndlovu pointed out in one of our panels last year, Africans have ALWAYS been writing genre literature – it's just that the publishing empires in Europe and North America have ignored it.

This interview first appeared on Lithub.
For the full interview, go to **https://lithub.com/readingafrica-five-writers-and-publishers-discuss-the-continents-boundless-literary-landscape/**

Jonathan Ball Publishers has three imprints:
*Jonathan Ball Publishers*, *Sunbird Publishers* and *Delta Books*.

Under these imprints, we publish in the following genres:

**South African non-fiction:**
*biography, history, business, military history and politics*

**Illustrated books about South Africa:**
*natural history, food, lifestyle and wildlife*

For more information, contact publishing director **Annie Olivier** at annie.olivier@jonathanball.co.za

Find our full catalogue here: https://www.jonathanball.co.za/download-our-catalogues/

For sales information contact **Kelly Ansara**
kelly.ansara@jonathanball.co.za or 011 601 8000

JonathanBall*Publishers*

# The End of an Era: Celebrating Three Vital African Presses

*by Colleen Higgs*

It is with sadness and a deep sense of appreciation that I note the closing of three important African presses. Two were owned and started by women, which for me makes their closure even more of a loss. They are Weaver Press, Blackbird Books and Huza Press. Each of them faced difficulties that they eventually could not overcome or were exhausted by. These include financial precarity, political turmoil, and unstable and harsh economic environments. And like other publishers, they had to contend with rising paper costs, piracy, dwindling donor and state funding and the worldwide shift away from reading books in favour of streaming, social media, gaming and other online activities.

**WEAVER PRESS** in Zimbabwe closed in December 2023 after celebrating 25 years of publishing, thus marking the end of an era in Zimbabwean publishing. It published novels, poetry, history, short stories, anthropology, memoirs, and environmental studies. Without Weaver Press, many of the most important Zimbabwean books would not have found their way into the world. From its office in Irene Staunton and Murray

McCartney's suburban home in Harare, Weaver Press launched the careers of numerous acclaimed writers, including NoViolet Bulawayo and Brian Chikwava.

We acknowledge the pivotal role that Staunton and McCartney played in growing Zimbabwean literature, bringing many authors to prominence. Weaver Press embodied the essence of Zimbabwe's evolving narrative, providing a platform for both established and emerging voices. Its legacy lives on in the books it brought to the world and the ongoing careers of the writers it first gave a home to.

# BLACKBIRD
BOOKS

**BLACKBIRD BOOKS**, a beacon of literary diversity in South Africa, is in the process of closing its doors to publishing new manuscripts after nearly a decade of groundbreaking work. Founded by Thabiso Mahlape in 2015, it has been a pioneering publishing house in the way it amplified black voices and unapologetically black stories in a post-apartheid landscape still grappling with inequality. As the first black woman-owned publishing house in South Africa, Blackbird Books challenged the status quo, nurturing new talent and inspiring confidence in emerging writers. Despite financial struggles and lack of state support, Mahlape's resilience and commitment to change has left an indelible mark on South African literature. Blackbird Books's legacy will inspire future generations of writers and publishers to fight for diverse voices in storytelling. The potential good news is that they hope to make a comeback soon. In the meantime, their books in print can be ordered from Protea Distribution.

Huza Press in Rwanda is closing its doors in December 2024. It has been a beacon of literary excellence in Rwanda and beyond since 2015. This visionary publishing house started by Louise Umutoni Bower has published diverse voices, nurtured talent and fostered a vibrant literary community. Huza Press's legacy will endure through the works it has brought to life, the writers it has championed, and the conversations it has sparked. From groundbreaking fiction prizes to innovative multimedia projects, such as RadioBookRwanda, Huza Press has redefined African publishing. Its impact on Rwanda's cultural landscape and the broader African literary scene will be felt for generations to come. We celebrate its contributions and the indelible mark it leaves behind.

\*

The closure of Weaver Press, Blackbird Books, and Huza Press marks a significant loss for African publishing. These pioneering publishers, each in their own way, have been instrumental in nurturing talent, amplifying diverse voices, and shaping the literary landscapes of Zimbabwe, South Africa, and Rwanda. Their impact extends far beyond national borders, contributing to the richness of African writing and publishing.

We recognize and celebrate their enduring legacies. Their closing gives us pause for thought and should encourage us to think of ways of making African publishing more sustainable. The authors they discovered, the stories they brought to light, and the conversations they sparked will continue to resonate for years to come.

# NEW CONTRAST LITERARY JOURNAL

*by Niamh Ahern and Robyn Paterson*

*New Contrast* has been providing a platform for South African writers since 1960. First established as *Contrast* by Jack Cope and, alongside *Upstream*, amalgamated into *New Contrast* in 1989, the literary journal was founded with the goal of providing "a flash-point for the vital currents moving everywhere" (Jack Cope). Now, in 2024, under the editorship of writer and poet Sindiswa Busuku, *New Contrast* returns to its initial impetus.

Since its inception, *New Contrast* has had the privilege of featuring many notable editors, such as Damon Galgut, Stephen Watson, Meg Vandermerwe, Michele Betty, Masande Ntshange, and Sihle Ntuli, as well as work by prominent writers, poets, and critics such as Breyten Breytenbach, Nadine Gordimer, Yvette Christiansë, Roneldia Kamfer, Karen Jennings, Wamuwi Mbao, and many more. Previous cover artists include Atang Tshikare, Pamela Phatsimo Sunstrum, Maureen Quin, and Adele van Heerden among others.

In addition to Sindiswa Busuku, Robyn Paterson (Managing Editor) and Niamh Ahern (Editorial Assistant) joined the editorial team in January. They are working alongside Megan Ross of the Stoep Collective (Production Designer), and Jennifer Pape (Web Designer), both of whom are long-time members of the *New Contrast* team.

We have historically published poetry and prose in many different South African languages. However, due to operational constraints, English was the primary language of publication in 2023, with inclusions of some isiZulu poetry. In 2024, we gained the capacity to reinstate a multilingual editorial team, and have appointed Shane van der Hoven and Paul Kammies as Afrikaans Editors and Mthunzikazi Mbungwana as isiXhosa Editor. *New Contrast* welcomes writing in various dialects of these languages, and we hope to expand the range of local languages included in the journal by expanding our editorial team. Whilst we are deeply committed to promoting local literature, we are equally passionate about platforming pan-African voices. We welcome submissions from writers across the globe.

In addition to poetry and prose, we are actively seeking out hybrid and genre-bending forms such as performance-based texts, lyric essays, and flash fiction. We are also developing our Criticism section by including work engaged in scholarship (literary and otherwise) in addition to book, music, art, and theatrical reviews.

Following the success of our launch of Issue 205 at Clarke's Bookshop in Cape Town, the current *New Contrast* editorial is excited to hold more in-person events, including readings, discussions, and performances. Our first foray into this territory was "Meditations on Silence", a poetry event that formed part of the *Open Book Festival* featuring readings by Zizipho Bam, Athambile Masola and Uhuru Phalafala.

You can submit to New Contrast by emailing **ed@newcontrast.net**.
Find out more about us by visiting our website **https://www.newcontrast.net** and following our Instagram **@new_contrast**

# #READING AFRICA

*by Jessica Powers*

When I launched Catalyst Press in 2017, I had a relatively simple goal: to publish African literature.

Unfortunately, simple goals become more complicated in real life.

Catalyst Press is based in both North America and South Africa. What this means is that marketing "African literature" to our southern African readership is easy, but we face challenges in North America.

For example, what is "African literature"? And…how do you get Americans to want to read it?

Is "African literature" defined as books written by African writers? Or does it include literature written about Africa? Is it only so-called serious literature that deals with themes that are germane in particular to the continent and its people? Or….is genre fiction by African writers "African literature"? That is, should a romance novel or a crime novel that happens to be authored by an African be defined as African literature or is categorized simply as a romance novel, a crime novel? And what about the diaspora, anyway? Is a person of African descent who lives in Great Britain and writes about African immigrants in Great Britain writing African literature or British literature? And this might make you feel a little bit crazy, but how do you define a novel written by an African that actually involves primarily American characters? Is that an African novel? Or is that an American novel written by an African?

Of course Africans don't need to have African literature defined for them. And most Africans probably don't care too much about whether the romance novel they're reading should be deemed "African literature" or just "a great romance that happens to be written by my cousin's neighbor down the street." And maybe they would and maybe they wouldn't be too interested in that novel written by an African that features primarily American characters.

But it is my unhappy duty to inform you that many people in my country think of "African literature" as "books that are written by Africans, books that are about Africans no matter where the book is set, books that are important only to Africans, and books that are primarily read by Africans." In general, they would see "African literature" as serious literature, read primarily by students in African Studies departments on our university campuses. It might never occur to them that genre fiction can be equally "African" and that a lover of romances might, after one or two tastes, just want to devour the romances being published on the continent.

So. The question of how to define "African literature" is pivotal to my publishing mission, second only to "how to get Americans to want to read it."

Enter #ReadingAfrica or #ReadingAfricaWeek, a weeklong online celebration of the breadth and diversity of books by African writers and about Africa.

Note that we call it "reading Africa," not "reading African literature." There's a reason for that.

I suppose you could say that #ReadingAfrica is trying to define "African literature" as broadly as possible. That would be true.

I suppose you could say that #ReadingAfrica is for the western world, but I don't think so. It's true that much of what we do during that week is trying to get people who don't already engage with African literature to engage with it.

But we want it to be for everybody.

We want this space, this week, to be a celebration of all books that are, in some way, derivative of Africa. In any genre.

So #ReadingAfrica is a growing, living, changing organism.

I grew up in El Paso, Texas. El Paso is 85% Mexican and Mexican-American. My parents are of European descent from the Midwest U.S. (the whitest part of the country.) I grew up as a "third-culture kid," meaning, my home culture was different from the culture that surrounded me. So I am always trying to bridge that gap. I'm always trying to make the exterior fit the interior.

What that means for #readingAfrica, which is a movement we would love to see taken up by other people and moved beyond our little sphere, is that we are trying to bridge the gap between outsider and insider. The insiders who already love "African literature" (however you define it) and the outsiders who aren't really sure what to make of it. The insiders who don't even think about "reading Africa" because it's already at least 50% of what they consume because it is, after all, their lives represented by those books – and the outsiders who haven't even considered whether these books could be relevant to their lives.

What I do know is that no matter where you are coming from, we want you to be involved. #ReadingAfrica occurs the first full week of December, rain or shine. We need ambassadors who will celebrate alongside of us on social media. We need audience members (readers, fans, booksellers, librarians, educators) who will come to the online events, and who will shine a light on African books and African writers wherever they live or work. We need authors and illustrators and publishers and agents to participate in the live events. No matter what your "position" is relative to the continent of Africa and to books that, in the broadest of possible definitions, somehow can be included in this vague term "African literature," we hope you'll come join us.

## THE ISLAND PRIZE

The Island Prize was founded in 2021 and is an annual prize for an unpublished novel by a debut novelist who lives in Africa or the diaspora. It was founded by Robert Peett of Holland House Books in the UK and Karen Jennings, a South African author, after her novel An Island was longlisted for the Booker Prize in 2021.

Karen has spoken publicly of the difficulty she has had in getting published. She remarks that "As African writers, we are often faced with a double dose of challenges. Firstly, getting published within African countries can be incredibly difficult because local publishers are often constrained by finances. Secondly, for many writers getting published overseas is almost impossible because the rest of the world has certain ideas of what an African story should be. Having experienced these challenges first-hand – being told that a novel is 'too African' or 'not African enough' – I know how important it is that stories from Africa be given a wide variety of platforms so that they can be shared at home and abroad without the need to fit certain moulds."

The Island Prize is focused on mentorship rather than prize money (which is very modest). The winning writer is supported in working on their manuscript and then in submitting it to agents and publishers. Mentorship is also offered to the two runners up.

The hope is that a prize like this can assist authors across the continent in gaining the confidence to tell stories as they wish and that, with time, such stories will become appreciated across the globe, without first being labelled as an exception or a surprise.

The submission period tends to be towards the end of the year.

Manuscripts must be previously unpublished (in any language) and the author cannot have published a novel before.

The manuscript should be between 35 000 and 100 000 words.

From left to right: Hamza Koudri, Sarah Isaacs and Reem Gaafar

## THE AERIAL PUBLISHING STORY

*by Cassandra Scheepers*

Aerial Publishing was born from an informal course in creative writing started at Rhodes University in 1997.

First about the course, which is known as the ISEA short course. It is still running, as a weekly two-hour evening class over 14 weeks, with much of the writing done in class. Initially independent, it was taken under the wing of the ISEA (Institute for the Study of the Englishes of Africa). The course is open to all members of the Grahamstown/Makhanda community, regardless of age or affiliation with Rhodes University. Since its inception, the course has 'graduated' over 350 people.

The methodology is based on the ideas of Paulo Freire, Peter Elbow, Natalie Goldberg, Christopher Vogler, and Louise Dunlap – encouraging trust and playfulness. Freire's emphasis on personal experience is important because, as one teacher put it, "People are more confident at expressing their most familiar experiences, such as relationships, dreams, work, and childhood memories."

Freewriting is a basic component of the course. One of the teachers, Carol Leff, has written:

> *One of the great things about freewriting is how it helps you shed notions that your writing is not good enough. You can write whatever you like, whether boring or shocking or incomprehensible: the only rule is that you keep writing.*

People always enjoyed the encouraging atmosphere:

*I looked forward to every Thursday evening. The coordinators provided a simple, open, supportive environment. The exercises were invigorating and shook my creative tree. There was sufficient scope to explore my own writing. A wonderful, enriching experience that has launched me into poetry writing. (Participant)*

*Looking back, the ISEA Creative Writing course offered me an opportunity to come out of the literary closet. It was when I shared my writing with other people for the first time. (Siphiwo Mahala, participant)*

Each year there were about 15-25 participants and three teachers. At the end of the year, some of the participants and teachers edited and published a magazine of the year's work called *Aerial*.

However, publishing a few poems and stories in an annual publication was not enough: some of the course participants had enough writing for manuscripts of their own. They approached the course teachers about how to get these published. The ambitions were modest – to publish books on a small scale, mainly for local readers. The teachers could also submit their manuscripts.

Thus, Aerial Publishing was formed, as a venture separate from the course. It was run as a collective, with a cooperative structure. Tasks were divided up between selecting which manuscripts to publish, editing the books, getting the books

Some copies of Aerial literary magazines, the anthologies and chapbooks.

designed and printed, as well as finances, sales and admin. After authors were published, they were expected to contribute their time and skills and participate in the collective in whatever way they could. The first books were printed in 2004, with seed funding from the Centre for the Book in Cape Town. They were sold via local launches and bookshops.

Twenty books have now been published, most of them poetry. The collective has been partially cost-covering, with some sponsorship and funding needed every few years.

In 2016, Aerial Publishing was formalised into a non-profit company, but it retained its cooperative character, and still called on its published writers to participate in choosing, editing and producing the books of newer writers.

No publishing was done during the 2020-2022 Covid hiatus, but during that time Aerial Publishing decided to do a selection from all the writing drawn from the annual course publication. This culminated in two anthologies released in

2024: *A Flower for the Dashboard: Poems from Aerial 1998-2019* and *The Last Time I Lived Anywhere Real: Stories from Aerial 1998-2019*, presenting work from multiple generations of the short course, by over 80 writers.

The anthologies are labours of love and reflect what happens when writers are driven by "stubborn faith and the love of poetry and stories" says the editor, Shirley Marais.

Meanwhile, Aerial Publishing lives on, as a small but effective example of community writing and publishing.

\*

To learn more about Aerial Publishing, and to get a pricelist of their books, contact aerial.publishing.makhanda@gmail.com.

The ISEA short writing course runs every year from March to August and continues to inspire new writers. If you are in or near Makhanda and want to join, contact isea@ru.ac.za.

www.ingramcontent.com/pod-product-compliance
Lightning Source LLC
Chambersburg PA
CBHW070334180426
43196CB00050B/2696